# DEACONS

Ministers of Christ and of God's Mysteries

Edited by Gearóid Dullea

Published 2010 by
Veritas Publications
7-8 Lower Abbey Street
Dublin 1, Ireland
Email publications@veritas.ie
Website www.veritas.ie

ISBN 978 1 84730 217 5
Copyright © Gearóid Dullea and the individual contributors, 2010

10 9 8 7 6 5 4 3 2 1

Unless otherwise indicated, all scriptural quotations are from the *New Revised Standard Version: Catholic Edition* (London: Geoffrey Chapman, 1993).
Unless otherwise indicated, quotations from texts of Vatican II are from *Decrees of Ecumenical Councils* (Norman P. Tanner, ed.), (London/Washington DC: Sheed and Ward/Georgetown University Press, 1990).

A catalogue record for this book is available from the British Library.

Designed by Norma Prause-Brewer
Printed in the Republic of Ireland by ColourBooks Ltd., Dublin

Veritas books are printed on paper made from the wood pulp of managed forests. For every tree felled, at least one tree is planted, thereby renewing natural resources.

# Contributors

**Donal McKeown** is Auxiliary Bishop in Down and Connor. He chairs the Bishops' Commission on Vocations and Pastoral Outreach to Youth and Third Level Students, and is a member of the Commission for Clergy, Seminaries and Permanent Diaconate.

**Diane Corkery** lectures in Scripture and is head of the Religious Studies Department at St Patrick's College, Thurles.

**Gearóid Dullea** is a priest of the diocese of Cork and Ross. He is Coordinator of the Formation Programme for the Permanent Diaconate.

**Thomas J. Norris** is a priest of the diocese of Ossory. He is Associate Professor of Systematic Theology, St Patrick's College, Maynooth, and a member of the International Theological Commission.

**Brendan McConvery CSsR** is a priest of the Redemptorist order. He is a lecturer in Scripture at St Patrick's College, Maynooth, and editor of *Scripture in Church*.

**Pádraig J. Corkery** is a priest of the diocese of Cork and Ross. He is head of the Department of Moral Theology and Dean of the Faculty of Theology in St Patrick's College, Maynooth.

**Patrick Jones** is a priest of the archdiocese of Dublin. He is the Director of the National Centre for Liturgy.

**William T. Ditewig** is a deacon based in Florida, USA, where he is Professor of Theology and Religious Studies at St Leo University, Tampa.

**Tony Schmitz** is a deacon in Scotland. He is Director of Studies on behalf of the Diaconate Commission of the Bishops' Conference of Scotland and co-editor of the *New Diaconal Review*.

# Contents

# Foreword

One of the key fruits of the Second Vatican Council (1962-1965) was the recovery of the role of all the baptised within the Church. All the baptised are called to exercise the gifts and duties that arise from their baptism. It is in that context that the Vatican Council's decision to restore the diaconate as a permanent and stable grade of the sacrament of Holy Orders (*Lumen Gentium* 29) is to be understood. For most people in this country Church ministry has been linked exclusively to priests. The introduction of the Permanent Diaconate in Ireland will require a radical re-evaluation of how we talk about and approach ministry in our Church.

With the Permanent Diaconate we are challenged to return to the sources of the lived expression of our faith - particularly sacred scripture and the living tradition of the Church - and appreciate the richness of the Church's insight into ministry among the people of God. This will become more important for the Church in Ireland as permanent deacons will be ordained in Irish dioceses over the next few years.

A deacon is ordained to assist the bishop, and work with his priests, as part of the threefold ancient ministry of the Church. The deacon's ministry has a triple focus: (a) of the word - proclaiming, preaching, and teaching; (b) of the altar - in liturgy; and (c) of charity - in the care of the poor and needy, in activating the social teaching of the Church, and in administration. Undoubtedly, as it takes root in the life of our Church, the deacon's ministry will adapt to the local particularities of the faith in this country while also learning from the experience of the diaconate in other countries.

As the Irish Church begins to develop an appreciation of the ministry of the permanent deacon, this book gives an introductory appraisal of much that will be useful to comprehend the diaconate and its implications. Its essays explore the scriptural, historical and theological backgrounds to the Permanent Diaconate, as well as the deacon's threefold ministry and the experience of the diaconate abroad. It may be a resource for parish pastoral councils and local presbyterates as they work towards the diaconate's introduction here. An enhanced understanding of the Permanent Diaconate will help ensure that its introduction in Ireland can revitalise all ministry in the Church so that the mystery of the One who took – and takes – the form of a servant may inspire ever more deeply all the Church's service.

**Dermot Farrell**
*National Director of the Permanent Diaconate*
*January 2010*

Bishop Donal McKeown

# The Permanent Diaconate: How Have We Come This Far?

## Background

In Ireland, it seems as if the first men to be ordained to the Permanent Diaconate will be taking up their ministry in the year 2012. They entered into their propaedeutic year in 2008 and in autumn 2009 started their three years of formal training leading to ordination. How has the Church in Ireland got to the stage where, for perhaps the first time ever in the country's Christian history, the decision has been taken to have men ordained to the diaconate, not as a stage towards priesthood but as a ministry in its own right with its own specific theology?

In 1996 there is evidence of the idea of the Permanent Diaconate being discussed at the Irish Episcopal Conference. Deacons have been playing an appreciable role in other countries for nearly forty years. In October 1996 the bishops formally discussed the Permanent Diaconate, and Irish members of the Liaison Committee (between the Episcopal Conferences of the UK and Ireland) were asked to discuss the issue with their colleagues in England, Wales and Scotland. At the March 1997 meeting, a document on the diaconate was circulated to bishops from the Archdiocese of St Andrews and Edinburgh.

In March 1998, Monsignor Denis O'Callaghan, who had been asked by the Episcopal Commission for Clergy, Vocations and Seminaries to prepare a report on the Permanent Diaconate, made a submission to the Bishops' Conference. Further discussions between the Commission, Monsignor O'Callaghan, and the Episcopal Conference of England and Wales took place throughout that year.

By March 1999, the bishops had decided that – after Monsignor O'Callaghan's consultations with bishops in both England and Wales and the USA – they would discuss the matter at length during the non-business meeting to be held in Rosslare in November that year. This discussion took place and the matter was to be further discussed at the March 2000 meeting.

The report of the March 2000 conference meeting suggests that the bishops recognised the need for some decision to be taken on the issue. A paper was circulated from Fr Roland Minnerath,[1] and the Commission for Clergy, Vocations and Seminaries was then asked to prepare a memorandum concerning a possible process of selection for candidates and a programme of formation so that a decision could be taken the following June.

At the October 2000 meeting, Bishop Patrick Walsh submitted a memorandum from the Clergy Commission. Following discussion, it was decided that 'in the light of the pastoral needs of the Church in Ireland, the Episcopal Conference considers it opportune to provide for the ordination of permanent deacons', and that 'in accordance with the provisions of *Lumen Gentium* 29b, the Episcopal Conference now seeks the approval of the Supreme Pontiff, John Paul II, for this decision.' The Clergy Commission was invited to prepare a memorandum on the proposed role and function of the permanent deacon and a catechesis for priests on the work of permanent deacons. Furthermore, Archbishop Neary would chair a committee to prepare a draft programme of formation.

This committee reported back the following March 2001 with a set of recommendations on selection, age limit, support structures, catechesis, etc. This was referred to the Doctrine Commission who reported back its satisfaction in June 2001. A decision was then taken to set up a new committee to look at the ministry and life of deacons in the country, while the Clergy Commission would prepare guidelines for the assessment of potential candidates.

By September of that year, initial responses from the Apostolic Nuncio and the Holy See were supportive of the idea and they invited the Conference to submit a set of Norms for recognition by Rome. A new committee – mooted the previous June – was then set up with a wider membership. It eventually consisted of eight members plus an Episcopal Chair, and included two lay people. Meanwhile Fr Kevin Doran was asked to co-ordinate the documentation from the Irish Church to ensure that it conformed to Vatican norms.

In June 2002, the draft National Directory on the Permanent Diaconate, prepared by Fr Doran, was examined by the Conference's Department of Catholic Education and Formation and was then discussed at the October meeting where a number of amendments were suggested. Two months later the document – now called *The Permanent Diaconate: National Directory and Norms for Ireland* – was approved for submission to the Vatican's Congregation for Catholic Education. In December 2004 certain modifications were requested by the Holy See and, with the acceptance of these amendments, the document was finally submitted to the Congregation for Catholic Education for *recognitio*. This was issued on 18 July 2005 and notified to the Conference at the September 2005 meeting. Ireland now had norms that could be used *ad experimentum* for a period of six years.

## Implementation stage

At the March 2006 meeting it was decided by the bishops that a Permanent Diaconate Working Party should be set up to deal with a variety of matters, specifically:

· A national catechesis of clergy and laity regarding the Diaconate;
· Norms for the selection and formation of candidates;
· The implementation of the Directory and Norms.

The relevant Episcopal Commission was also asked to begin discussions with Maynooth in relation to an appropriate programme of formation and academic training.

The Working Group, chaired by Bishop Donal McKeown, met on five occasions over the next number of months. Input to its work came from Fr Ashley Beck, Director of Diaconate Formation in the Archdiocese of Southwark (who addressed the December

2006 Episcopal Conference meeting) and from other members of the Advisory Board of the Commission for Pastoral Renewal and Adult Faith Formation. A straw-poll of the bishops in October 2006 had indicated that about fourteen dioceses were considering the possibility of introducing the diaconate.

The Working Party recommendations were brought to Conference for the March 2007 meeting and proposed:

- That any national catechesis take place in the context of a wider catechesis on ministry. To that purpose, a two-day workshop was organised for early summer 2007;
- Before candidates are selected for formation, that a catechesis should take place at diocesan level, along the lines indicated in *Restoring the Permanent Diaconate: Practical Questions to be Addressed in the Irish Context* and drawing on *National Directory and Norms*;
- That particular emphasis be placed on developing an understanding of the Permanent Diaconate among the diocesan clergy, who will be called upon to work closely with the deacons, and who will be primarily responsible for helping the faithful to understand the diaconate, and inviting suitable candidates to come forward;
- That a brochure on the Permanent Diaconate, prepared by the working group, be used to support the catechetical process at diocesan level;
- That the Episcopal Conference appoint a National Director for the Permanent Diaconate;
- As the approval of the *National Directory and Norms* is for a six-year period, beginning in summer 2005, that the process of evaluation and revision begin by 2009.

The bishops agreed that the working party would prepare job descriptions for any future national director and director of the propaedeutic year. In June 2007 Monsignor Dermot Farrell was appointed as National Director for the Permanent Diaconate.

In October 2007 the programme for the propaedeutic year for candidates was approved and in December 2007 Monsignor Farrell presented to the bishops four documents in relation to various aspects of the diaconal ministry, selection of candidates, and the various dimensions of formation.

When the bishops met in June 2008 they appointed, for a three-year period, Fr Gearóid Dullea as Co-ordinator of the Formation Programme for the Permanent Diaconate. They also decided that local ordinaries should be able to make decisions during the *ad experimentum* period about whether to accept candidates into formation after they had reached the upper age limit of sixty.

One final piece of the jigsaw remained to be put in place. In March 2009 the Conference meeting established the National Training Authority in accordance with paragraph 52.1 of the *National Directory and Norms*. Membership would include:

- Bishop Francis Lagan;
- the President and Dean of the Faculty of Theology of St Patrick's College, Maynooth;
- the National Director of the Permanent Diaconate;
- the Co-ordinator of the Formation Programme for the Permanent Diaconate;
- the President of Mater Dei Institute of Education;
- Bishop Donal McKeown (Chair).

That body met for the first time on 16 June 2009 to consider submissions for formation of permanent deacons – one from St Patrick's College, Maynooth, and one from the Dublin Centre for Formation in Ministry, based at Mater Dei. Subject to some proposed amendments, both of these programmes were accepted as suitable and approved for a period of three years.

And thus the stage was set for the first Permanent Diaconate formation in Ireland. It had taken almost thirteen years from when the idea was first raised at a meeting of the Irish Episcopal Conference.

What might be remembered from the process?

· Inspiration for new ideas can come from any part of the People of God. In this instance it came from many quarters, including letters from the faithful, contact with other Episcopal Conferences, and reflections by various thinkers.

· The Permanent Diaconate cannot be seen in isolation but rather in the context of current ecclesiology and theology of ministry.

· Ideas take a period of time to mature. Thus diocesan and national discussions and catechesis are necessary if a new initiative is to be introduced. It is a deficient ecclesiology which assumes that the People of God – and the presbyterate – can simply have something new foisted on them without preparation.

· Much learning can be gained from other neighbouring countries where deacons have been in existence for many years.

· Things happen best when specific people are given either a programme of work to prepare for subsequent meetings or national responsibilities.

NOTE
1. Roland Minnerath is a Member of the Pontifical Theological Commission. A lecturer in Church History in the Faculty of Theology in Strasbourg, in 2004 he was ordained Archbishop of Dijon.

Diane Corkery

# The Scriptural Roots of the Diaconate

## Introduction

The Greek term *diakonos* (translated as 'servant', 'minister', or sometimes 'deacon') and the associated terms *diakonia* ('service') and *diakoneō* ('to serve') are used by New Testament authors to describe the proliferation of Christian ministries and functions within the nascent Christian movement. This is indicative of the reality that a deeply ingrained sense of service permeated the collective consciousness of the early Christians. Paul, for example, depicts his foundational work and Apollos' subsequent ministry among the Corinthian community using the metaphor of servanthood: 'What then is Apollos? What is Paul? Servants [*diakonois*] through whom you came to believe, *as the Lord assigned* to each' (1 Cor 3:5; emphasis added). On many occasions, the apostolic ministry of the Twelve, of Paul and of their many collaborators is portrayed using the language of service. These early evangelists are regularly called 'servants of Christ and stewards of God's mysteries' (1 Cor 4:1), 'servants of this Gospel' (Col 1:23) and 'ministers of a new covenant' (2 Cor 3:6). **From even an initial survey of the New Testament, there is a sense that *diakonia* is somehow the heart and foundation stone of all Christian ministries and for this reason an examination of the scriptural roots of the diaconal ministry can never be dislocated from an understanding of the New Testament concept of service.**

This essay leads to a crucial insight and caveat that is well worth bearing in mind right from the outset: one should not expect to find in the texts of the New Testament a generic model that later defined the diaconal ministry. It is interesting that the New Testament is largely circumspect when it comes to a more formalised diaconal ministry. The International Theological

Commission's historico-theological research document on the Permanent Diaconate perceptively explains that while ministries were beginning to take shape in the Church, 'the terminology of these ministries was not yet fixed'.[1] In a similar vein, Wayne A. Meeks explains, 'No group can persist for any appreciable time without developing some patterns of leadership, some differentiation of roles among its members ...'[2] In a very positive way the New Testament bears witness to the process of formalising roles and offices. It is also apparent from a reading of the New Testament that 'the early Church attributed the formation of the various ministries to the action of the Holy Spirit (1 Cor 12:28; Eph 4:11; Acts 20:28) and to the personal initiative of the apostles, who owed their sending forth on their mission to the Most High ... (Mk 3:13-19; 6:6-13; Mt 28:16-20; Acts 1:15-26; Gal 1:10-24)'.[3] This is positively demonstrated below by a reading of the appointment of the seven Greek men in Acts 6:1-6, who are commissioned by the Apostles (Acts 6:6) on the basis that they are 'full of the Spirit and of wisdom' (Acts 6:3). Indeed, this may be a template for the appointment of believers to ministerial roles within the community. It is with this backdrop in mind that we now turn to the New Testament in an attempt to capture the vision of *diakonia* that lies therein, with the hope of gleaning some significant insights into the nature of the diaconal ministry.

## The *Diakonia* of Christ and his Followers in Mark

Of fundamental importance is the reality that the New Testament authors describe Christ's ministry and mission in terms of the verb *diakoneō* ('to serve'). Having provided a model of leadership (Mk 10:42-44) contrary to what some of the disciples of Jesus might have expected (Mk 10:35-37), the Markan Jesus declares, 'For the Son of Man came not to be served but to serve, and to give his life a ransom for many' (Mk 10:45; cf. Mt 12:18). John N. Collins, in *Deacons and the Church*, carries out a thorough investigation of these words of Jesus in Mark's gospel.[4] Through a careful analysis, and paying attention to grammar and syntax, Collins restructures Mark 10:45 in an alternative fashion. He places the punctuation after the passive verb 'to be served' and before the conjunction 'but' and, therefore, the verse reads as follows: 'For the Son of Man came not to be served, *but to serve and to give his life a ransom for many.*' The latter half of the verse in italics is, as Collins explains, 'self-contained and contains a full and free-standing idea: "the Son of Man came to serve by giving his life a ransom for many".'[5] Looking at Mark 10:45 from this particular angle, the ministry of Jesus designated by the verb *diakoneō* has little to do with Jesus' compassionate ministry to the poor, the lame and the marginalised, and more to do with *serving God*. Jesus' service from this perspective is carrying out God's will to the point of death or, as Francis J. Moloney puts it, 'self-giving unto death, so that others might have life'.[6] What inspiration might a deacon today take from this reading of Mark? **In imitation of Jesus, service is self-sacrificial in nature and is always in relation to the will of God.**

The opening part of Mark 10:45 ('the Son of Man came not to be served') allows for another essential insight into the nature of Jesus' ministry. Jesus' kingship is not comparable with other socio-political patterns of leadership. Jesus is not a despotic leader like many of the Roman emperors, endowed with glory and honour and having a cortège of attendants waiting on him. Instead, his leadership is characterised by a giving up of an already ascribed right 'to be served'. There is a sense that Mark 10:45a could be read as follows: 'For the Son of Man came not to be served (*even though that was his right*).' By giving up his right to be served or, at the very least, by coming 'not to be served', Jesus inverts conventional patterns of leadership. The disciples are to imitate Jesus' model of leadership. This is made explicit in Mark 10:42-44, when Jesus explains: 'You know that among the Gentiles those whom they recognise as their rulers lord it over them, and their great ones are tyrants over them. But it is not so among you; but whoever wishes to become great among you must be your servant [*diakonos*], and whoever wants to be first among you must be the slave [*doulos*] of all.' Life as authentic disciples of Jesus in the Kingdom of God is only achieved through the abandonment of society's means of acquiring honour (through imperial greatness in the Markan example) and through serving God with a self-sacrificial internal disposition (in imitation of the Markan Jesus).

## The *Diakonia* of Christ and his Followers according to Paul

The Christ-hymn of Philippians 2:6-11 discloses that Paul was thinking along similar lines as the author of Mark's gospel in relation to the nature of Christ's mission and the reality of modelling one's life on Christ himself. Taking this hymn as a kind of spiritual map, Paul insists that the Philippians are to put on the mind of Christ: 'Let the same mind be in you that was in Christ Jesus' (Phil 2:5). The significance of the hymn for Paul is underscored by Michael J. Gorman in his assertion that the hymn 'should be called not merely the centrepiece of Philippians, but Paul's master story'.[7] **The reality of this hymn is that exaltation, glory and honour worthy of a genuine leader and/or disciple comes about through the imitation of Christ's self-emptying and self-humbling disposition:** 'though he was in the form of God, did not regard equality with God as something to be exploited, but emptied himself, taking the form of a slave, being born in human likeness. And being found in human form, he humbled himself and became obedient to the point of death – even death on a cross' (Phil 2:6-8). Taking into consideration the cultural echoes of the hymn, Christ's example stands in stark contrast to self-glorifying Roman emperors (who were thought of as being in the form of God) and the Roman pursuit of honour.[8] Bearing in mind the intertextual links, particularly with the story of the first man Adam in Genesis 2-3, Christ's example is in contrast to the self-exalting Adam, who was also in some sense in the 'form' or 'image' of God.[9]

On many occasions in the epistles Paul offers himself as a role model for the Christian life. Such an appeal finds genuine credibility only because his own life is an imitation of Christ: 'Be imitators of me, as I am of Christ' (1 Cor 11:1). Michael J. Gorman, sensitive to Paul's language and story, provides two examples of how Paul imitates the mindset of Christ expressed in the Philippians' hymn.[10] Both autobiographical examples follow the pattern of the Philippians' hymn. In relation to 1 Thessalonians 2:6-8, Gorman explains that 'Paul depicts his behavior as "although [x] not [y] but [z]" when he says that "although we [x] might have thrown our weight around as apostles, we did not [y] seek honour from humans, but we [z] were gentle among you and were pleased to share with you, not only the gospel, but our own selves".[11] His behaviour follows the pattern of Christ, who even though [x] he possessed equality with God, did not [y] take advantage of this for self-edification, but [z] emptied and humbled himself through the incarnation and through the acceptance of death. **From Paul's perspective, the Christian life and, indeed, all Christian ministries find their essence in relation to Christ's self-emptying mission at the service of others.**

## Service of the Poor and the Word – The Acts of the Apostles

The Acts of the Apostles – Luke's second volume – also has an insight to offer on the diaconal ministry. The story of the selection of seven Greek men in Acts 6:1-6 has been traditionally conceived of as a story about the election of the first deacons.[12] The appointment of the seven was prompted by the Apostles' pronouncement: 'It is not right that we should neglect the Word of God in order to wait on tables (*diakoneō*)' (Acts 6:2). Many scholars who have presented exhaustive studies of the diaconal ministry, including James Monroe Barnett and John N. Collins, conclude that these seven men, who have been specifically selected for the purposes of 'serving at tables' (Acts 6:2) and to partake in 'the daily distribution [of food?]' (Acts 6:1), were not deacons per se.[13] This assertion is reinforced by the observation that the Greek noun for deacon, *diakonos*, is not used in relation to the seven. **A reason, however, for the conventional tendency to view this passage as foundational for the diaconal ministry might be due to Luke's use of** *diakon* **words on three occasions.** He describes 'the distribution' to the Greek widows (Acts 6:1) and the Twelve's 'service' of the word (Acts 6:4) by using the Greek noun *diakonia*. The Greek verb *diakoneō* is used in reference to serving tables in Acts 6:3.

In addition, the traditional inclination to identify the seven as deacons might account for the misconception that the deacon's role was primarily that of loving service to the needy, if their role is conceived of in terms of the distribution of food to the widows. Care of the poor was certainly a prerogative of the Jerusalem Church. Earlier on in Acts, Luke explains in relation to the Christian community at Jerusalem: 'There was not a needy person among them, for as many as owned lands or houses sold them and brought the proceeds of what was sold. They laid it at the apostles' feet, and it was distributed to each as any had need' (Acts 4:34-35). Interestingly, the Greek word used for distribution here is *diadidōmi*, which makes the connection with the distribution (*diakonia*) in Acts 6:1 slightly more tenuous (this might be significant for an alternative interpretation of Acts 6:1-10 below). Because the numbers within the community were increasing this may have led to the neglecting of the widows at the distribution. Some scholars suggest that the Greek widows might be specifically overlooked because of internal disputes between Aramaic- and Greek-speaking Jewish Christians.

**Of prime importance is the reality that service or** *diakonia* **in the Acts of the Apostles is fundamentally associated with the apostolic mission to spread the word of the Lord abroad.**[14] The suggestion that the Greek widows have been neglected in the 'distribution' (*diakonia*) could mean that they were being overlooked in the daily 'distribution' of the word. Acts of the Apostles attests to the fact that much of the Jerusalem ministry of the Apostles took place within the confines of the Jewish Temple (cf. Lk 24:53; Act 3:10, 5:20-21). If these Greek-speaking widows attended gatherings in the Temple forecourts then they would not have been able to understand these Aramaic-speaking preachers. The same would apply to gatherings in a household context.

With this backdrop in mind, the Twelve's declaration, 'It is not right that we should neglect the Word of God in order to wait on tables' (Acts 6:2) brings about a very different understanding. Collins provides a useful summary of his overarching interpretation of this passage when he asserts that, 'the Hellenists' widows were in need of preachers who could teach them in Greek, and preferably at home when Greek speakers came together at their tables (6:2).'[15] That these seven men were engaged in the ministry of the word rather than ministering at table or ministering to the poor is corroborated by the activities of Stephen and Phillip in the wider narrative of Acts.[16] Stephen delivers a lengthy discourse in the synagogue in Jerusalem prior to his martyrdom (Acts 7), and Phillip's ministry in Samaria is also characterised by proclaiming the word and indeed by baptising people (Acts 8).

The importance of Acts 6:1-6 for the renewal of the Permanent Diaconate today does not lie in establishing the fact that this story is about the first deacons in the community of believers and the specific nature of their role. Whether or not the seven men are deacons is not the point of the story. Whether the role of the seven has to do with the distribution of the bread or the distribution of the word to the neglected Greek widows in Jerusalem is a literary-historical concern. The value of this story for an appreciation of the diaconal ministry today lies in the fact that it testifies to the importance of identifying and taking on board the needs of a community of believers and proactively selecting members 'of good reputation, filled with the Spirit and with wisdom, to whom we can hand over this duty' (Acts 6:3). **The renewal of the Permanent Diaconate today is in the spirit of the Apostles' recognition of the necessity to remain focused on their own apostleship by appointing others to roles of responsibility in response to the needs of the community.**

## Deacons at Philippi

In correspondence with the church at Philippi around AD50, Paul extends a greeting 'to all the saints in Christ Jesus who are in Philippi, with the bishops and deacons' (Phil 1:1). Even though this opening address suggests that a more formal role of deacon was operative in the community, it is anachronistic to view the role through the lens of a more developed office that inevitably emerged in the history of the Church. The same applies to the role of the *episkopoi* ('bishops' or 'overseers') in Philippians 1:1. Paul, assuming that his audience is familiar with the activities of these functionaries, gives no redundant details concerning who the deacons were and what specifically their role entailed. The opening verse, however, offers certain insights into the nature of the role of the *diakonoi* ('deacons'). Of fundamental importance is the reality that Paul singles out the *episkopoi* and the *diakonoi* together for a special address. There is something quite instinctive about Paul's placing of these two categories of people side by side. **Furthermore, the sequential placement of the *diakonoi* after the *episkopoi* in this opening greeting suggests that the deacons' role is somehow defined in relation to the *episkopoi*.**

Collins, having carried out an extensive study of the use of the term *diakonos* in Greek literature, and therefore cognisant of the reality that a *diakonos* never stood alone, explains that 'whenever there is a *diakonos*, somewhere in the background is a person or group of people to whom the *diakonos* is responsible in the carrying out of a task. By definition the *diakonos* stands in relation to someone else who has mandated a task to the *diakonos*.'[17] This explanation fits with the description of Phoebe's role in Romans 16:1: 'a delegate (*diakonos*) of the church in Cenchreae.' Phoebe (not a 'deaconess' as some English translations suggest) has been mandated to a specific task and, therefore, Paul refers to her as a *diakonos*. The nature of her task is open to interpretation, but she may well have been the bearer of the epistle or is using her considerable influence as a 'patron' to conduct religious business. In light of this, it is quite reasonable to assert that the *diakonoi* in Philippians were religious assistants and operated under the mandate of the *episkopoi*. The deacons may have been involved in the collecting and sending of the gift to Paul under the bishops' authorisation, for which he shows appreciation in Philippians 4:16-18. Interestingly, this may have been the reason why Paul singles out the 'bishops and deacons' for a specific greeting.

The role of the *diakonoi* at Philippi might also have entailed functions at religious ceremonies, particularly in relation to the Lord's Supper celebrated in the communities founded by Paul (cf. 1 Cor 11:20ff.). This is supported by a survey of Greek sources, where the title *diakonos* was used to refer to those who 'performed as waiters at religious festivals that included meals'.[18] Paul's community of believers in the Greco-Roman city of Philippi could quite naturally have adopted this familiar title to speak of those who performed duties at the Eucharistic celebration. This is in some way consistent with the use of the term *diakonos* within the context of the Last Supper in the Gospel of Luke 22:26-27. Indeed, we may well have arrived at foundational evidence for the role of the deacon at liturgical celebrations, particularly in relation to assisting during the Eucharistic liturgy.

## Deacons in the First Epistle to Timothy

In comparison to the New Testament sources explored so far, 1 Timothy allots considerably more space to a discussion about deacons within the community, although the author's concerns relate more to the virtues of the deacon rather than a description of the role (1 Tim 3:8ff.). Barnett, in explaining that 'most of the New Testament information regarding the office is to be found in 1 Timothy 3:3-18', envisages a more structured role of deacon within the community. Collins also acknowledges a more formalised role when he notes that the term for deacon 'does at last take on the air of a title belonging to an institution'.[19]

The fact that the specific tasks of the deacons are not described implies that the functions of the deacon were established and understood by the community. The author's main concern is to find suitable candidates to take up the position. Significantly, the role is a means by which one can receive great acclaim, given that the author explains, 'for those who serve well as deacons gain a good standing for themselves and great boldness in the faith that is in Christ Jesus' (1 Tim 3:13). Furthermore, the core virtues of the bishop and the deacons are expressed with the same underlying sentiment, indicating that the deacons were held in high esteem within the Church. Similar to the opening address in Philippians 1:1, the deacons find distinction in relation to the figure of the bishop (*episkopos* appears in the singular in 1 Timothy) and probably operate under the mandate of the bishop. A period of training to assess their capabilities appears to be an essential part of the appointment process: 'And let them first be tested; then, if they prove themselves blameless, let them serve as deacons' (1 Tim 3:10). This is directly related to the preceding description of the deacons' fundamental attributes in 1 Timothy 3:8-10.

Even though the author remains silent about their specific roles, scholars attempt to reconstruct their historical functions by picking up on the undertones of the epistle. Clare Drury, for example, perceives that the roles of the bishop and the deacons may not be 'dissimilar except for a greater emphasis on management and teaching in the case of the *episkopos*'.[20] Collins suggests that 'the role of deacons was confined to assistance of the *episkopos* in connection with the gathering of believers and with any common meal upon that occasion'.[21] The prospect that some of the earliest deacons assisted at the Eucharistic meal comes into view once again.

## Conclusion

The renewal of the diaconal ministry relies heavily upon a successful understanding of the New Testament's vision of service. As we have seen above, contemporary scholarship on the diaconal ministry cannot ignore what a relatively recent report by the Church of England calls the 'rediscovery of the biblical idea of *diakonia*'.[22] The publication of John N. Collins's *Diakonia: Reinterpreting the Ancient Sources* led to the realisation that the New Testament concept of *diakonia* is not solely to be understood as service to the poor or the needy, a type of Christian social work.[23] Collins's study counterbalances a temptation to give too much weight to the loving and caring service aspect of the deacon's ministry when constructing a theology of the diaconal ministry and, for that matter, in pastoral training. Collins explains that 'the only reason an early Christian would have designated social work as [*diakonia*] would have been [...] that social work was understood to be one more among the set of responsibilities that the gospel lays on the Christian.'[24] The Roman Catholic Church's renewal of the Permanent Diaconate with its threefold ministry of word, altar and charity is in harmony with the scriptural vision of service that cannot simply be confined to the loving service of the poor that characterised one aspect of Jesus' ministry. While the New Testament vision of *diakonia* can never be cut off from the ministry of charity, it is much richer than simply serving the needy. The International Theological Commission's research document on the Permanent Diaconate succinctly captures the essence of *diakonia* in its assertion that 'Being a Christian means following Christ's example in putting oneself at the service of others to the point of self-renunciation and self-giving, for love.'[25]

NOTES

1 *From the Diakonia of Christ to the Diakonia of the Apostles*, International Theological Commission Historico-Theological Research Document, London: Catholic Truth Society, 2003, p. 5.

2 Wayne A. Meeks, *The First Urban Christians: The Social World of the Apostle Paul* (2nd ed.), New Haven: Yale University Press, 2003, p. 111.

3 *From the Diakonia of Christ*, p. 5.

4 John N. Collins, *Deacons and the Church: Making Connections Between Old and New*, Pennsylvania: Morehouse, 2002, pp. 28-39.

5 Ibid., p. 32.

6 Francis, J. Moloney, *The Gospel of Mark: A Commentary*, Peabody, MA: Hendrickson, 2002, p. 208.

7 Michael J. Gorman, *Inhabiting the Cruciform God: Kenosis, Justification, and Theosis in Paul's Narrative Soteriology*, Grand Rapids, MI: Eerdmans, 2009, p. 12.

8 Ibid., p. 19.
9 Ibid., pp. 13–16.
10 1 Thess 2:6-8; 1 Cor 9.
11 Gorman, *Inhabiting the Cruciform God*, p. 23.
12 See Irenaeus, *Against Heresies* 3, 12:10.
13 The translation of the Greek (*en tē diakonia*) varies significantly across English translations of the Bible: 'in the daily ministration' (*King James*); 'in the daily distribution' (*New Jerusalem*); 'in the daily distribution of food' (*New Revised Standard Version*).
14 Collins, *Deacons and the Church*, pp. 52–4.
15 Ibid., p. 57.
16 Luke is silent about the ministry of the other five men, but it can be assumed that their ministry is along the lines of that of Stephen and Philip.
17 Collins, *Deacons and the Church*, p. 89.
18 Ibid., p. 90.
19 Ibid., p. 98.
20 Clare Drury, 'The Pastoral Epistles' in *The Oxford Bible Commentary*, John Barton and John Muddiman (eds), Oxford: Oxford University Press, 2001, p. 1225.
21 Collins, *Deacons and the Church*, p. 101.
22 'For Such A Times As This: A Renewed Diaconate in the Church of England', Report to the General Synod of the Church of England of a Working Party of the House of Bishops, London: Church House Publishing, 2001, p. 9.
23 John N. Collins, *Diakonia: Re-interpreting the Ancient Sources*, New York: Oxford University Press, 1990.
24 Ibid., p. 254.
25 *From the Diakonia of Christ*, p. 3.

Gearóid Dullea

# The Development of the Diaconate

## Introduction

The emergence and development of the diaconate in the sub-apostolic period and the patristic era is quite well documented and has much background material. Indeed the diaconate has many references from the life of the early Church. The purpose of this essay is to present some of these details in such a way that will enable us to see the diaconate as an intrinsic part of the Church's ministry arising organically from the scriptural accounts and growing into a clearly discernible office in the first centuries of the life of the believing community.

The scriptural evidence of deacons is not negligible even if details regarding the functions that they exercised are minimal. While there are intimations of a diaconal nature in the gospel accounts, such as the 'service' orientation of all leadership, it is really in the Pauline corpus and other New Testament writings that a more well-defined picture is given (Rom 16:1; Phil 1; 1 Tim 3). **From these insights the *diakonos* is linked closely with the *episkopos* and there is a strong apostolic dimension to the diaconate.**

## Early Witnesses

At the end of the first century/beginning of the second century the Didache gives prominence to the diaconate. The *diakonos* has a function of teaching and prophecy; he is a close associate with the *episkopos*, possibly having a leadership role in the life of the church. 'Appoint for yourselves therefore *episkopoi* and *diakonoi* worthy of the Lord, men who are meek and do not have love of money, and who are true and approved; for they also perform to you the service of the prophets and teachers. Therefore do not scorn them; for they are your honourable men, along with the prophets and teachers.'[1] This source is especially important given the early date for the composition of the text as well as the fact that it was closely associated with other writings that were eventually accepted into the scriptural canon. It has clear resonances of the reference in Philippians 1:1: 'To all the saints in Christ Jesus who are in Philippi with the *episkopoi* and *diakonoi.*'

This view of the *diakonos* is corroborated by the writings of Clement of Rome and Ignatius of Antioch, who see the *diakonos* linked with the *episkopos*. In his letter written towards the end of the first century to the Corinthian Church addressing a dispute concerning leadership of the community, Clement asserts the apostolic foundations of bishops as rulers of the Church: '... it had been written concerning bishops and deacons from very ancient times; for thus says the scripture in a certain place, I will appoint their bishops in righteousness and their deacons in faith.'[2]

**For Ignatius the ministry of the deacon is 'the ministry of Jesus Christ'.** 'I exhort you to study and to do all things with a divine harmony, while your bishop presides in the place of God, and your presbyters in the place of the assembly of the apostles, along with your deacons, who are most dear to me, and are entrusted with the ministry of Jesus Christ.'[3] The diaconate is part of the ordered structure of the Church from the time of the Apostles. Ignatius elaborates on this point by seeing the *diakonos* as a co-worker with the *episkopoi* and *presbyteroi*. **He finds it unthinkable that the Church would exist without this threefold ministry** and he gives us one of the early formulations of what would later be termed as the three grades of the sacrament of Holy Orders. 'In like manner let all men respect the deacons as Jesus Christ, even as they should respect the bishop as being a type of the Father and the presbyters as the council of God and as the college of Apostles. Apart from these there is not even the name of a church.'[4] He also mentions some of the particular functions of the deacon in the liturgy: he is minister of the chalice; he proclaims the gospel; he announces parts of the Eucharistic celebration; and he serves the entire *ekklesia*. He also envisages deacons having a legatine or representative function within the community.[5]

Around AD140 the *Shepherd of Hermas* speaks expressly of the administration of alms for the poor. This concern with the material needs of the poor and vulnerable will recur in much of the later writing on the diaconate and, indeed, is one of the three basic foci of a deacon's ministry – word, altar and charity. Speaking reproachfully of unfaithful deacons the writer says, 'They that have the spots are deacons that exercised their office ill, and plundered the livelihood of widows and orphans, and made gain for themselves from the ministrations which they had received to perform. If then they abide in the same evil desire, they are dead and there is no hope of life for them; but if they turn again and fulfil their ministrations in purity, it shall be possible for them to live.'[6]

Polycarp (d.155) understands the role of the deacon as one of leadership, serving as part of the local ruling council. Even though he does not mention *episkopoi* in his letter he still exhorts deacons to virtuous living as they are 'deacons of God and Christ and not of men; not calumniators, not double-tongued, not lovers of money, temperate in all things, compassionate, diligent, walking according to the truth of the Lord who became a *diakonos* of all.'[7]

From the Church's incipient interaction with the Greco-Roman culture of the time the apologists attempted to give a reasonable account of the new faith. **In his tradition we have Justin Martyr who gives more information regarding the liturgical functions of a deacon**: he distributes Holy Communion, administers the chalice and brings the Eucharist to the absent.[8] Interestingly here the deacon is a servant of the Church's communion – a clear link between the building up of the Church and the liturgical life of the community.

## Ongoing Developments

It is Irenaeus (c.130–c.200) who makes the first stated and unambiguous connection between the 'Seven' of Acts 6 and deacons in the Church when he refers to Stephen as the first deacon chosen by the apostles.[9] There is a rich theological vein to all of this as he roots Church order in the Apostles, a decisive factor in later thought on the Church's fundamental organisation.

At roughly the same time the *Pseudo-Clementines* make a rather memorable reference to deacons as the eyes of the bishop in all matters, but especially in identifying the needs of the people. The sick have a particular right to the deacon's ministry and he is called to keep order in the *ekklesia*.[10]

Tertullian mentions the deacon's prerogative of baptising, akin to the priest's.[11] There is further elaboration on the ordination of deacons and on their liturgical ministry from Hippoloytus.[12] He precisely elaborates the deacon's ordination in the following terms: 'In the ordination of a deacon, only the bishop lays on his hand, because the deacon is not ordained to the priesthood, but to the service of the bishop, to do that which he commands',[13] a statement that would have a lasting impact on the Church's understanding of the diaconate.

Written probably in Syria c.235 the *Teaching of the Twelve Apostles (Didascalia Apostolorum)* develops the early *leitmotiv* of the connection between the bishop and the deacon. The deacon is to be 'the hearing of the bishop, and his mouth and his heart and his soul'.[14] His relationship with the bishop is to be equivalent to that of a father and son. With the bishop and priests he administers justice and he has specific functions in the liturgy such as announcing the Prayer of the Faithful. He speaks of the bishop as sitting 'in the place of God Almighty. But the deacon stands in the place of Christ'.[15]

Pope Fabian (d.250) divided the city of Rome into seven districts entrusting the administrative functions of each area to deacons. The story of the deacon Lawrence, who died in 258, fits into this context.[16]

Again around the middle of that century Cyprian speaks of the deacon's concern for the poor, especially with regard to the administration of the Church's resources. Interestingly, he mentions deacons as extraordinary ministers of reconciliation, an aspect of the deacon's ministry that is not much developed later on. This, he averred, was to be exercised by the deacon in the absence of the *presbyteros*.[17]

In Origen deacons have a duty to preach.[18] On a more prosaic level Jerome notes that deacons are better paid than priests and he also ascribes to them the function of blessing the paschal candle at Easter.[19]

## Conciliar and Later Interventions
In conciliar legislation we see a streamlining of the deacon's ministry. There is a greater level of regulation regarding what deacons could and could not do. At Elvira in c.306, while deacons could head small rural communities, the function of taking Holy Communion to the sick was to be done only with the bishop's permission.[20] At Arles (c.314) he was expressly forbidden to preside at the Eucharist and his ministry was to be exercised only with the knowledge of the priest.[21] Nicaea in 325 reiterated the ban on a deacon presiding at the Eucharist and located the deacon's position as below that of the presbyter.[22]

With the growing significance of the presbyter in the Church the position of the deacon declined concomitantly. There are also some references in Ambrosiater and Jerome to problems emerging, with deacons being accused of boastfulness and pushiness.[23] It is difficult to say how widespread this perception was but in any case the importance of the diaconate was clearly waning. The relationship between presbyters and deacons was never clearly defined, something that some maintain was a cause for the decline of the diaconate throughout the middle ages.

Late in the fourth century the *Apostolic Constitutions* set out in some detail the liturgical functions of the deacon. He is to announce the various stages of the Eucharistic celebration and lead the prayers of the faithful, proclaim the gospel, represent the bishop at synods in his absence, assist at baptisms, welcome newcomers, etc.[24]

Augustine saw deacons having an important role in catechetics. In a letter to a deacon called Deogratias he speaks of his 'rich gift in catechising'.[25] A significant elaboration came in c.475 when *Statuta Ecclesiae Antiqua* spoke of deacons being ordained *'non ad sacerdotium sed ad ministerium'*.[26] (Many centuries later this reference will be found in *Lumen Gentium 29*). However it is clear that deacons were subordinate to bishops and presbyters and this reflects a mutation of Hippolytus' assertion that the deacon was ordained *'in ministerio episcopi'*.

John Chrysostym reiterated this differentiation between bishops and priests on the one hand and deacons on the other.[27] Pope Leo the Great (d.461) treated of the tasks of deacons among which he mentioned mediator, ambassador, and particularly significant in the context of the council of Chalcedon in 451, representative at councils.[28]

There are scattered references to deacons in the subsequent centuries such as at the Council of Toledo in 633 which made legislation regarding them.[29] Writing in the mid-eleventh century Peter Lombard repeated the traditional teaching on deacons: the role was primarily that of assistants to priests and they mainly had liturgical duties.[30] Thomas Aquinas evaluated the diaconate in relation to the priesthood, especially in the *potestas* of the priest at the eucharist. Consequently for him the deacon was located between the priest and the subdeacon and his duties were ceremonial.[31] One also notes personalities like Pope Gregory VII (d.1085) who was elected bishop of Rome while still in deacon's orders. Other noteworthy deacons were Saint Francis of Assisi who played a pivotal role in the twelfth-century reform of the Church, and Cardinal Reginald Pole as a papal legate at the Council of Trent.

## The Tridentine View

In September 1562 the Council deliberated on the sacrament of Holy Orders. It is in this context that during the summer of 1563 the Council of Trent discussed the diaconate with a remarkable degree of sensitivity to the possibilities that existed for this ministry. Various positions were advanced ranging from discussions to prevent deacons from engaging in preaching to proposing a set period of time for deacons to function before their ordination as priests. **In fact there were some calls for the ('pristine') diaconate of the patristic age to be restored.** The *Acta* record a particularly full and comprehensive view of the diaconate during a debate in July 1563 that spoke of deacons as 'the eyes of bishops ... [a ministry that has special regard for] widows, students, orphans, the imprisoned, the sick, and all afflicted'.[32] Throughout these debates there was of course an overriding concern to articulate the Church's doctrine and discipline on the episcopate and the priesthood. Eventually the council in its twenty-third session taught that the diaconate and minor orders are all connected to the priesthood.[33] There is no evidence that this provision was acted on. (Indeed during the Vatican II debate in October 1963 on the restoration of the diaconate, Cardinal Julius Döpfner of Munich claimed that the Vatican II proposal was more wary and cautious than the view of the diaconate at Trent.)[34]

The theological opinion of theologians from the post-Trent era (e.g de Victoria and Bellarmine) tended towards an affirmation of the sacramentality of the diaconate, although there was no absolute unanimity on this matter. The canonical structuring that was put in place in the 1917 *Code of Canon Law* did however regard a deacon as a cleric but its provisions were mainly set out only insofar as a deacon would eventually be ordained a priest.[35]

## Backdrop to Vatican II

Therefore, until Vatican II the diaconate remained primarily a stage on the programme of preparation for the priesthood – a stage that was temporary and, largely speaking, liturgical. It was only at Vatican II that the diaconate was definitively re-established in its own right as a permanent ministry in the life of the Church. Yet the decision of Vatican II to renew the diaconate did not occur in a vacuum. There was much ferment in and development of theology of orders, the place of the lay apostolate, the understanding of the Church, the fresh insight of scripture and the patristic tradition, as well as a keen awareness of the pastoral needs of the mission of the Church. This is the background to the teaching that found its supreme realisation in *LG 29*. There were undoubtedly many factors that influenced the decision of the Council Fathers at Vatican II. Some consideration is now given to these trends.[36]

The first of these was the theological developments regarding the diaconate carried out mainly in Germany prior to World War II. Particularly salient in this regard were the articles that appeared in the journal of the *Deutscher Caritas Verband*, an 1897 creation of the German Catholic bishops charged with the duty of charitable outreach to those in need. **These articles called for the social mission of the Church to be endowed with a sacramental root in order to strengthen the work of the Church with sacramental grace and solidify the connection between word and sacrament.** These moves would be seen as a credible response by the Church in responding to the needs of the world as well as strengthening the role of the episcopate because of the deacon's special link to the bishop.

The second trend may be termed the Dachau experience and post-war developments in Germany. While imprisoned in Dachau concentration camp some German clergy began to articulate a new presentation of ministry. Notable here was the work of Fr Wilhelm Schamoni and Fr Otto Pies which was subsequently published in the German journal *Stimmen der Zeit*. There was also a growing reflection being carried out by other interested individuals, something which eventually grew into the International Diaconate Circle. This meant that there was **much thought and background material available to the Council Fathers at Vatican II.** Of immense importance was the 1962 work by Karl

Rahner and Herbert Vorgrimler, a book of articles on the history, theology and possibilities for the diaconate.[37]

The new thought being given to the possibility of a renewal of the diaconate drew inspiration from a third source: the opinion that a renewed diaconate would play a large role in primary evangelisation in mission territories. This opinion was given strong impetus and development at a number of International Catechetical Study weeks that took place between 1959 and 1968. The catechetical focus of this work was bolstered by an important text by the French priest Michel-Dominique Epagneul, 'Du role des diacres dans l'Église d'ajourd'hui', published in 1957.[38] This article saw deacons being associated in a special way with the work of priests.

The fourth important source that fed the renewal of interest in the diaconate was papal teaching from the 1940s and 1950s. Pope Pius XII's *Sacramentum Ordinis* unambiguously located the diaconate as part of the sacrament of Holy Orders and it went on to teach definitively what the matter and form of this sacrament were.[39] At the Second World Congress on the Apostolate of the Laity held in Rome in 1957 he went on to speak of the growing thought on the establishment of the diaconate but he noted that the time was 'not yet ripe'.[40] This address gave new vigour to the reflections on the diaconate, all of which eventually gave a new impetus to the debates at Vatican II.

## Conclusion

This brief essay has charted the developments through the centuries of the diaconate. From its emergence in the early Church to its consolidation and growth through the patristic period though its eclipse in the middle ages and its reinstatement at Vatican II, the diaconate emerges with a strong body of historical evidence. Needless to say, Vatican II's decision regarding the diaconate may not be cast simply as a restoration of the ancient diaconate of the early Church; from this survey, neither may it be regarded as an extraneous interpolation without a basis in the ministerial tradition of the faith.

## NOTES

1 *Didache* 15:1-4.
2 I Clement 42:5.
3 Ignatius, *Magnesians* 6:2.
4 Ignatius, *Trallians* 3:1.
5 Ignatius, *Philadelphians* 10:1.
6 *The Shepherd of Hermas* 16[103]:2.
7 Polycarp, *Philippians* 5:2.
8 Justin Martyr, *First Apology* 65:2.
9 Irenaeus, *Against the Heresies* 3, 12:10.
10 See Ps-Clement, *Homilies* 3.67; *Epistle to James* 12.
11 Tertullian, *On Baptism* 17.
12 See Hippoloytus, *Apostolic Tradition* 8; 9; 21.
13 Ibid., 8:1-2.
14 *Didascalia Apostolorum* 11 [ii, 44].
15 Ibid., 9 [ii, 26].
16 For a brief version of Saint Lawrence's life and ministry, see Owen F. Cummings, *Saintly Deacons*, Mahwah, NJ: Paulist Press, 2005, pp. 17-23.
17 Cyprian, *Epistle XII* (12).
18 Origen, *Homilies on Joshua*.
19 Jerome, *Epistle* 28.
20 Elvira, canons 32 and 77.
21 Arles, canons 15 and 18.
22 Nicaea, canon 18.
23 See *Ambrosiaster* 101.5; Jerome, *Letter to Evangelus* 146.1.
24 *Apostolic Constitutions* book 2 and book 8.
25 Augustine, *On Catechising of the Uninstructed* 1.1.
26 *Statuta Ecclesiae Antiqua* 4.
27 John Chrysostom, *Homily 11* (preaching on 1 Tim 3:8-10).
28 Leo I, *Letters* 34.
29 Council of Toledo, canons 27 and 58.
30 Peter Lombard, *Sentences* 4 dist. 24.10.
31 Thomas Aquinas, *Summa Theologiae Supplementum Tertiae Partis*, q. 37, art. 5 ad 5.
32 *Concilium Tridentium* 9.601(report of a text considered on 6 July 1563).
33 See *DS* 1765, 1772.
34 Vatican II, *Acta Synodalia*, II/II, 227-230.
35 *Code of Canon Law* (1917), canons 738; 845; 1094; 1146; 1274§2; 1333.
36 See J. Hornef and P. Winninger, 'Chronique de la restauration du diaconat (1945-1965)' in Paul Winninger and Yves Congar (eds), *Le Diacre dans l'Église*, Paris: Cerf, 1966, pp. 205-222. Also Edward P. Echlin, *The Deacon in the Church; Past and Future*, New York: Alba House, 1971.
37 Karl Rahner and Herbert Vorgrimler (eds), *Diaconia in Christo: Über die Erneuerung des Diakonates, Quaestiones Disputatae* 15/16, Freiburg: Herder, 1962.
38 Published in *Nouvelle Revue Théologique* 79 (1957), pp. 153-168.
39 Apostolic Constitution, *Sacramentum Ordinis*, 30 November 1947, *Acta Apostolicae Sedis* 40 (1947), 5.
40 Pius XII, 'Quelques aspects fondamentaux de l'apostolat des laïcs: Hiérarchie et Apostolat', *Acta Apostolicae Sedis* 49 (1957), p. 925.

Thomas J. Norris

# Deacons – Servants of Communion

## A Perspective

In 2003 the International Theological Commission (ITC), after many years of research, published its document on the Permanent Diaconate.[1] Founded by Pope Paul VI three years after Vatican II, the Commission has the purpose of facilitating cooperation between the magisterium of the Church and theologians. This type of cooperation had been quite obvious during the work of the Council. **The work of the ITC is intended as a *diakonia* to the magisterium on the part of the theologians.** The title of the document is *From the Diakonia of Christ to the Diakonia of the Apostles*. The text seeks to read the documents of the council and the post-conciliar magisterium dealing with the Permanent Diaconate.

To begin with, there is a particular perspective to be found in *Lumen Gentium*, the *magna carta* of the entire council. As we now realise, *LG* proposes a deep and comprehensive understanding of the Church. To recognise this, one need only look at the sequence of the chapters. The first chapter presents the Church as mystery, the second as the People of God, the third chapter looks at the hierarchical structure with particular reference to the episcopate. The council emphasises the fact that the Church is 'a people made one by the unity of the Father, Son and the Holy Spirit'.[2] The Church, then, is not primarily a hierarchical organisation but a living reality. Indeed, Saint Irenaeus of Lyons speaks of the 'ancient organism of the Church'.[3] In the words of Klaus Hemmerle, 'The Church is the created heaven of the Trinity, while the Trinity is the uncreated heaven of the Church'.[4] For this reason the Church is also 'as a sacrament or instrumental sign of intimate union with God, and of the unity of all humanity'.[5] This underlines the urgent necessity of having categories capable of expressing this originality. These categories should bring out a vision of the Church as the 'divine-human' communion of humanity with the Blessed Trinity, and of humanity in unity.

It is only in the third chapter that the hierarchical structure of this communion-Church appears. Here one sees immediately the theme of unity-communion in its doctrine of the collegiality of bishops with the pope as the successor of Peter and, therefore, as the foundation of their visible unity in the world. One encounters again the Trinitarian categories as means for understanding the seal of the Triune God on the earthly pilgrim Church. It is in this context that we encounter the conciliar doctrine on the diaconate.

It is not surprising therefore that in the paragraph preceding that on the diaconate the council spoke of this unity in the following fashion: 'Since today the human race is moving together more and more towards civil, economic and social unity, it is that much more necessary that priests, by their united care and resources, under the leadership of the bishops and the supreme pontiff, wipe out every cause of division so that the whole human race may be brought into the unity of God's family.'[5] This is similar to the opening lines of the constitution itself. **Priests, and *a fortiori* deacons, must above all be men of communion and therefore workers for the unity desired by Christ (see Jn 17:21f.).**

In this perspective there is another extremely important dimension: the Christological dimension. Christ brought on earth the life of the Triune God. 'I came that they may have life and have it abundantly' (Jn 10:10). He has not only brought this life but also 'taught' it. In fact, his love, which goes all the way to the cross (Jn 13:1; Gal 2:20; Eph 5:2), shows the 'how' of living, not only according to this new life but also in and from this new life. It is necessary to live for the other. You are more important than I am! Jesus showed a God who did not spare his only Son but gave him up for all of us (Rom 8:32). And so he has invited all of us, 'Love one another as I have loved you' (Jn 13:34, 15:12).

This perspective is emphasised from the beginning of the ITC document. The text says, 'Through the incarnation of the word who is God and by whom all was made (cf. Jn 1:1-18) the strangest revolution imaginable has come about. The *Kyrios*, Lord, become the *diakonos*, servant, of all. The Lord God comes out to meet us in his servant Jesus Christ, the only Son of God (Rom 1:3), who, being in the "form of God", "did not see in the form of God a prize to be coveted, but emptied himself, taking the form of a slave. Having become like men … he abased himself and became obedient to death, even death on a cross" (Phil 2:6-8).'[7] Christianity is a revolution! And it is a revolution because its founder is a revolutionary: he becomes the *diakonos* of all. As the Apostolic Father, Polycarp, says, 'The Lord has made himself servant of all.'[8] Therefore there is a christological stamp on all dimensions of ecclesial life. This stamp contains an informative as well as a performative role: the Son who has lived the *kenosis* revealed that 'God is love' (1 Jn 4:8, 16). **The essence of Christianity is learned only from the *diakonia* of Christ.**

Otherwise one does not understand any more the Christ who 'stripped himself' and 'humbled himself' even 'unto death, death on a cross'. Every brother or sister that I meet is my Lord! I am his *diakonos*! Only the person who seeks to live like this is a Christian. This is so because, as *Gaudium et Spes* says, 'It is only in the mystery of the Word incarnate that light is shed on the mystery of humankind' (22). This leads to the consequence that, 'the human … can attain its full identity only in sincere self-giving' (*GS* 24). *'Amo, ergo sum'* is the truth of human existence revealed to us in Jesus the Son of God who became the Son of Man! The Fathers of the Church loved to say that the most wonderful thing that could ever happen to a human being was to receive the grace of becoming a Christian and of living like one.

## Reading the Texts of Vatican II

'A theological approach to the diaconate in the wake of Vatican II should start from the council texts, examine how they were received and how they were later enlarged upon in the documents of the Magisterium, take account of the fact that the restoration of the diaconate was accomplished very unevenly in the post-conciliar period, and above all, pay special attention to the doctrinal fluctuations which have closely shadowed the various pastoral suggestions.'[9] Therefore we begin immediately with a reading of the conciliar texts, a work well done in the document from the ITC. **It is necessary to notice that the relevant conciliar references are numerous (cf. *SC* 35; *LG* 28, 29, 41; *OE* 17; *CD* 15; *DV* 25; *AG* 15, 16), a fact that shows the growing importance of the theme during Vatican II.**

This importance is not easy to understand. The Permanent Diaconate was an institution that was in abeyance for more than a millennium in the Church. Why did an interest in it emerge with real vigour at the council? **The answer has to do with the experience of the Church after the war and also with the intentions of the council itself.** It must be remembered that many bishops felt profoundly the lack of priests in some places to serve the People of God. The council debate, however, unfolded more slowly, more on a pastoral level than on a doctrinal level. The council fathers saw that the diaconate was something that could give a new importance to the priesthood.

The theological basis for the restoration of the diaconate took on a particular focus. Some fathers underlined the fact that the diaconate formed part of the nature of the Church from the beginning (*LG* 28a). The restoration then would not be a change but the return of an element that was present from the start but had been lost sight of along the way. Some fathers emphasised the fact that the diaconate formed part of the sacrament of Order and therefore should be renewed. Perhaps they were remembering the words of the martyr, St Ignatius: 'Let everyone revere the deacons as Jesus Christ, the bishop as the image of the Father, and the presbyters as the senate of God and the assembly of the apostles. For without them one cannot speak of the Church.'[10] *LG* 29 proposed the 'circumstantial reasons' which were determined by the council. 'Vatican II foresaw deacons engaging in tasks (*munera*) which were very necessary to the life of the Church (*ad vitam ecclesiae summopere necessaria*), but which in many reasons could be fulfilled only with difficulty because of the discipline of the Latin Church as it existed at the time. The present difficulties caused by the shortage of priests demanded some response. Care for the faithful (*pro cura animarum*) was the determining factor in re-establishing the Permanent Diaconate in the local Church. The re-establishment of the Permanent Diaconate was therefore intended to respond to pastoral needs which were grave, not merely peripheral ones.'[11] Therefore priests were not required to fulfil all of the tasks for the life of the Church.

The Decree on the Missions, *Ad Gentes*, draws attention to more reasons for its restoration. 'There were already men who were in fact exercising the diaconal ministry.'[12] In fact between *LG* and *AG* there took place a certain change in intention within the council itself. By the imposition of hands, deacons would be able to exercise their ministries strengthened by the grace of the sacrament. As the ITC put it, 'Finally, it was a confirmation, a reinforcement and a more complete incorporation into the ministry of the Church of those who were already *de facto* exercising the ministry of deacons.'[13]

**The doctrinal vision of the council consists above all else in the teaching that 'for the nourishment and continued growth of the People of God, Christ the Lord instituted in his Church a variety of ministries, which are directed towards the good of the whole body' (*LG* 18a).** Like the other sacred ministers, deacons are to consecrate themselves to the growth of the Church and the pursuit of its plan of salvation. Bishops who possess the fullness of the priesthood, presbyters as their co-operators in the sacerdotal ministry, and deacons exercise one ecclesiastical ministry in hierarchical communion. Distinct according to the will of Christ, one must remember that in the thinking at Vatican II the mission of all sacred ministers is to nourish the People of God and lead them towards salvation.

## A New Context: The Experience of the Post-Conciliar Permanent Diaconate

At the time of Vatican II the Permanent Diaconate had, as we have seen, a strongly pastoral aspect. Today this pastoral aspect has gained in significance because some local churches have acted on certain conciliar decisions. Given the fact that according to the council it was the duty of bishops joined with the Universal Pastor, the Pope, to decide whether or not to restore the Permanent Diaconate in local churches, the Church has learned much in recent decades. At the same time the *sensus fidei* of the People of God has been able to search more deeply into the ecclesial tradition. Therefore it is appropriate to look at the lived experience of the Permanent Diaconate after the council, as is done in the sixth chapter of the document of the ITC.

As the ITC says, one can recognise two typical situations of the Permanent Diaconate. The first consists of local churches where there are few deacons, while the second involves local churches where there are many deacons. The statistics show a great contrast. Directly after the council many thought that the Permanent Diaconate would be the solution to all sorts of pastoral problems in Africa and South America. However, it was the opposite that came about: there are few deacons in Africa and Latin America while the greater number of them is found in the USA and in general in western Europe.

How is one to understand this, especially when one remembers that the debate at Vatican II held the opposite view? In the young Churches there are catechists who provided, and are still providing, an outstanding *diakonia* in their local communities. Bishops have not promoted the Permanent Diaconate in these circumstances. Because of the diminution of the numbers of priests in the West, however, bishops have promoted the Permanent Diaconate. In both situations, pastoral needs have been the 'circumstantial reasons' even though the council fathers wished to restore the Permanent Diaconate for reasons of faith, namely, to show the original tripartite ministry given by Jesus Christ to the Apostles to journey on earth towards the eschaton.

## The Post-Conciliar Magisterium

The concrete situation of the Permanent Diaconate in today's Church, where it seems that permanent deacons can be understood solely as assistant ministers to priests, constitutes a new challenge for a true doctrine and understanding of the diaconate itself. This challenge is the necessary and relevant context if one is to read correctly the teaching of the post-conciliar magisterium on the diaconate.[14] We will now proceed to examine the principal directions of this teaching.[15]

A first line of enquiry has to consider the sacramentality of the diaconate. 'The most reliable doctrine and that most in accord with ecclesial practice is that which holds that the diaconate is a sacrament.'[16] This is the point of departure for other doctrinal elements. Sacramentality finds its roots in Christ although this truth would not necessarily demand that Christ himself had 'instituted' the sacrament. Instead, 'The cautious language used by Trent (*divina ordinatione*) and Vatican II (*divinitus institutum ... iam ab antiquo*) reflects the impossibility of totally identifying Christ's and the Church's activity with relation to the sacraments, and also reflects the complexity of the historical facts.'[17] **While the Council does not mention the sacramental character of the diaconate as an integral part of the sacrament of Order, *Sacrum diaconatus ordinem* does mention it.** This, however, does not resolve all theological difficulties. There is, for example, the question as to how one distinguishes the sacramental character of the deacon from that of the priest.

The bishop and the priest act *'in persona Christi capitis'*.[18] In the conciliar texts, however, this phrase is not applied to diaconal ministry but this language does emerge in post-conciliar documents.[19] Theologians have discussed its validity without reaching unity on the matter. In general, the *'specificum'* of the diaconate ought to be distinguished from the *specificum* of the episcopate and priesthood. Perhaps one possible way to achieve this would be **to recognise the** *specificum* **of the deacon** **'in** *persona Christ Servi'.* The deacon would then be an icon of Christ the servant of the entire human race. In *LG* 29a one finds a specification which teaches that deacons receive the imposition of hands 'not for the priesthood but for the ministry'.[20] In general one can say that bishops and priests have the *'potestas conficiendi eucharistiam et absolvendi et ...'*

## A Theological-Pastoral Context: The 'Ecclesiology of Communion'

In Vatican II we encounter an extraordinary maturity in the area of ecclesiology. Two of the four conciliar constitutions seek to present the mystery of the Church. The ecclesiology that emerges from this is regularly described as 'an ecclesiology of communion'. This is particularly the case since the synod of 1985. 'This ecclesiology grants a clearer understanding of the Church as a "universal sacrament of salvation" (cf. *LG* 1) which finds in the communion of the Trinitarian God the source and ecclesial model for all the dynamism of salvation. *Diakonia* is the realisation of this model in history. It now remains to be seen how the specific sacramental configuration of the diaconal ministry is integrated within this *diakonia* as a whole.'[21]

According to the ancient teaching of the Church, the teaching of Vatican II, and the post-conciliar magisterium, the diaconate includes a number of functions exercised according to varying and variable priorities. How can we arrive at a synthesis as to the identity of the deacon? This must be seen in the context of the communion of the Church, for whom the deacon is called to be a man of this lived communion. One can see this communion specified according to the classical *tria munera*, namely, that deacons 'serve the People of God in the ministry of liturgy, of preaching, and of charity' (*LG* 29a). From this one can propose a **tripartite** **communion as constitutive of a deacon's life: communion with** **Jesus in the Eucharist, in the word and in one's brother or sister.**

The deacon meets the risen Christ in the Eucharist. 'Those who eat my flesh and drink my blood abide in me and I in them' (Jn 6:56). As 'the sacrament of love, the sign of unity and the bond of charity',[22] the Eucharist makes the many into one body. The sacramental body constitutes the mystical body (cf. 1 Cor 10:16-17) The deacon whose *diakonia* is fulfilled especially in the ambit of the Eucharist ought to become ever more a 'man of communion' so that his life is coherent with what he does in the liturgy.

Second, the deacon carries out the *diakonia* of the word. But he must first meet the Logos-made flesh for all people in his word, since the word is a presence of the crucified and risen Lord. It is a word of divine life (cf. Phil 2:16) which nourishes the divine life in the heart of the believer and *a fortiori* in the deacon. Before preaching the word to others he should be the one who has not only heard the word but also put it into practice (Jam 1:22-25).

According to revelation, each person 'is the brother or sister that Christ died for'. Jesus lives in each brother and sister, a fact that is a hinge of revealed faith so that what we do for another person is in reality done for Christ (cf. Mt 25:30-45). Given that Christ is in each brother and sister, the deacon is under the imperative to love Jesus in all. Jesus 'loved us first' (1 Jn 4:19) and so deacons have the clear imperative to imitate him who loved first.

This threefold communion of the deacon – with Jesus in the Eucharist, with Jesus in the word, and with Jesus in the brother/sister – helps him to be 'planted in love and built on love' (Eph 3:17). Thus the deacons, or better, Jesus working through the deacons, gradually become more equipped for their *diakonia* of the People of God. They live as men of communion before exercising the three *munera* which have as their very *raison d'être* the upbuilding of the Church as communion. And given the fact that according to John Paul II the greatest need of the Church in the third millennium is 'to make the Church the home and the school of communion',[23] the vocation of deacons has a particular beauty, namely, living as men of communion they build the Church-communion which answers God's plan and responds to the world's deepest yearning.

NOTES

1 International Theological Commission Historico-Theological Research Document, *De la diaconie du Christ à la diaconie des apôtres* (2002). Quotations here are taken from the translation given in *From the Diakonia of Christ to the Diakonia of the Apostles*, London: Catholic Truth Society, 2003.

2 *LG* 4.

3 Irenaeus of Lyons, *Adversus Haereses I*, 4:33

4 Klaus Hemmerle, 'Trinitarische Kirche – Kirche als Communio' in *Gemeinsam für die Menscheit*, Neue Stadt Dokumentation 2, Munich, 1988, 53.

5 *LG* 1.

6 *LG* 28.

7 *From the Diakonia of Christ*, p. 3.

8 Polycarp, *Philippians* 5:2.

9 *From the Diakonia of Christ*, p. 72.

10 St Ignatius of Antioch, *Letter to the Trallians*, 3, 1; see also *Letter to the Smyrnaeans*, 8, 1.

11 *From the Diakonia of Christ*, p. 58.

12 Ibid., p. 59.

13 Ibid.

14 See the American study 'National Study of the Diaconate, Summary Report' in *Origins*, Vol. 25, No. 30 (18 January 1996).

15 The main documents are: Paul VI, Motu Proprio *Sacrum diaconatus ordinem* (1967); Apostolic Constitution *Pontificalis romani recognitio* (1968); Motu Proprio *Ad Pascendum* (1972); the new *Codex Iuris Canonici* (1983) and the *Catechism of the Catholic Church* (1992, 1997).

16 *From the Diakonia of Christ*, p. 73.

17 Ibid., p. 75.

18 For bishops see *LG* 21b; for priests see *LG* 10b.

19 E.g *Code of Canon Law* (1983), canon 1008. This canon has been modified by Pope Benedict XVI's Motu Proprio *Omnium in Mentem*, issued on 15 December 2009.

20 Here *Lumen Gentium* is quoting from Hippolytus, *Apostolic Tradition* 8:1-2.

21 *From the Diakonia of Christ*, p. 94.

22 *SC* 47.

23 *Novo Millennio Ineunte* 43.

Brendan McConvery CSsR

# The Deacon and the Ministry of the Word

During the liturgy of ordination to the diaconate, the bishop hands the Book of the Gospels to the newly ordained deacon saying, 'Receive the Gospel of Christ, whose herald you now are. Believe what you read, teach what you believe, and practice what you teach.' This short formula sums up admirably the deacon's relationship to the Word of God.

## The Deacon as Proclaimer of the Word

When a deacon takes part in the celebration of the Eucharist, it belongs to him by the right he has received through ordination to proclaim the gospel to the assembly, just as it is the right of the presiding bishop or presbyter to preach the homily. **The impression can sometimes be given that the homily is the high-point of the Liturgy of the Word. It is not. It is the proclamation of the Word of God itself from the scriptures of the Old and New Testament by those who share a sacramental responsibility for proclaiming the word to their brothers and sisters.** The first responsibility, through baptism, belongs to the readers who proclaim the readings from the Old Testament and the Apostles. It is the deacon's right through his order to proclaim the gospel. The liturgy has surrounded the proclamation of the gospel with special solemnity – a procession in which the Book of the Gospels is borne by the deacon from the altar to the lectern accompanied by song, lights and incense, the incensing of the Book of the Gospels prior to the reading and the veneration of the Book of the Gospels at the end of the reading. These are not mere optional extras to be reserved for a few solemn occasions in the year: they are part of the liturgical language of signs that highlights the centrality of the gospel in every celebration.

A friend told me recently that an elderly concelebrant at a weekday Mass she had attended read the gospel with such conviction and enthusiasm that it was evident how much he believed it. Reading a scriptural text, no matter how familiar it may be, demands hard work and preparation. The reader must ask himself or herself – how can I make this text live? Preparing a text for reading is not simply a matter of scanning it quickly to see if there are any hard words that are likely to trip you up as you read. The *General Introduction to the Lectionary* insists on the need for readers to be trained so that 'the faithful may develop a warm and living love for Scripture from listening to the sacred texts read'. While the *Introduction* regards spiritual preparation (at least a biblical and liturgical formation) as a prerequisite, it also highlights the need for 'a technical preparation' which makes the readers 'more skilled in the art of reading publicly', including the proper use of amplification systems.[1] While speaking primarily about liturgical readers, this advice applies with equal validity to all, including deacons, who exercise a ministry of the word. The reader (and deacon) should spend much of the preceding week becoming familiar with the text. Early encounters with the text might ask the question: what kind of text is this? Is it a narrative about Jesus, a parable that Jesus is telling, a challenging saying? Some sense of the literary form will help the reader to address the next step in preparation: how am I going to communicate this as Word of God to the congregation by the way in which I read it? This will include the basics such as noting the punctuation marks – differences between a comma, full-stop, and question mark, for instance. A more important question is how can the reader/deacon communicate the rhythms, tensions and power of this text to the assembly? While not attempting to act a part, this kind of engagement with the text gives its proclamation a unique authority.

## The Deacon as Preacher of the Word

In the liturgical homily of the rite of diaconal ordination, the ordaining bishop tells the congregation that, among the other responsibilities of the deacon, 'it will also be his duty, at the bishop's discretion, to bring God's word to believer and unbeliever alike'. The older Code of Canon Law (1917) had recognised the deacon's role as a preacher (canon 1342) but since diaconate was for the most part a transitional ministry assumed for a relatively brief time by those preceding to priestly ordination, it gave it very little attention. By contrast, the revised Code recognised that 'it is also for deacons to serve the people of God in the ministry of the word in communion with the bishop and his *presbyterium*' (canon 757). A deacon possesses the faculty for preaching everywhere, unless it has been restricted or taken away by the diocesan bishop (canon 764).

The liturgical homily delivered in the course of the community's celebration of the Sunday Eucharist sets the standard for all other preaching, even if it is not the only form of preaching. While he may not be the regular preacher at the Sunday assembly – that still remains the primary obligation of the pastor – the deacon may on occasion act as homilist by reason of his office. Good preaching, like good reading, demands preparation. **Since the homily is a 'breaking of the word' that corresponds to the 'breaking of the bread' later in the liturgy, the preacher needs to spend time engaged with the word through study and prayer.** First and foremost, the formation of the preacher requires a solid grounding in biblical study. The preparatory formation course for both presbyters and deacons should provide the beginnings of such a grounding, but learning more about the Bible, and especially about the gospels, requires a life-long commitment to biblical study. The Roman lectionary, by organising the readings in a three-year cycle, suggests immediately one help to this life-long process of learning. Engaging with an up-to-date commentary on the gospel of the year is an excellent way of engaging in systematic scriptural study. There are other aids to study including homiletic journals such as *Scripture in Church* that provide some basic tools that help the preacher engage with the texts.

The Swiss Protestant theologian Karl Barth advised his students when they were preparing a sermon to 'take your Bible and take your newspaper and read both but interpret newspapers from your Bible'. **A homily is not an exercise in biblical or textual archaeology. It is an engagement with the Word of God, which is alive and active, that demands to be spoken to the minds and hearts of people today and to elicit a response from them.** Modern society is so saturated by media coverage and advertising that it is demanding in what it expects. Good preaching must engage the mind. It demands care – care in crafting language, care in clothing what are often abstract ideas in the flesh of narrative and human experience. It demands too, as Barth says, that the events of the everyday world be interpreted in the light of faith. If liturgical preaching is to achieve its purpose, the preacher also needs to be familiar and in tune with the ebb and flow of the seasons of the liturgical year since it is through the liturgy that the saving mystery of our salvation is made actual. 'Throughout the liturgical year, but above all in the seasons of Easter, Lent and Advent, the choice and sequence of readings are aimed at giving the faithful an ever-deepening perception of the faith they profess and of the history of salvation.'[2]

There are times when the deacon will be on his own as preacher. They may include the celebration of those sacraments or liturgies in which he is the presiding minister – baptism, marriage, funerals, Sunday or weekday celebrations of the word, when it is not possible to have a full parish Eucharist. In virtue of his presiding role, the deacon is the ordinary preacher at such events. If it would be wrong to see the deacon as a substitute or second-best celebrant on such occasions, it would be equally wrong to see the deacon as 'a second string preacher'. Deacons are ordained to fulfil the office of preaching, and the proclamation of the word is an essential part of the sacramental celebration.

## The Deacon as Teacher of the Word

The third aspect of the deacon's service to the word is the deacon's responsibility as a teacher of the word. It will come in many forms. A first likely area is preparation especially for what we might call the sacramental milestones of baptism, first communion, confirmation and marriage. An important part of that preparation will be the choice of scriptural texts to be used in this particular celebration. **Helping the participants to choose and especially to 'own' their chosen texts as an expression of the faith they profess in the celebration offers a moment of encounter around the word.** Pope Benedict has commented on how this engagement with people in the preparation for the sacrament helps them 'to reflect more deeply on the mystery of the divine life that has been given to us.'[3]

Catechesis also falls within the deacon's ministry of the word. The *Catechism of the Catholic Church* defines catechesis as 'the totality of the Church's efforts to make disciples, to help men believe that Jesus is the Son of God so that believing they might have life in his name, and to educate and instruct them in this life, thus building up the body of Christ.'[4] Speaking later of the privileged place of scripture in catechesis, the *Catechism* says: 'such is the force and power of the Word of God that it can serve the Church as her support and vigour, and the children of the Church as strength for their faith, food for the soul, and a pure and lasting fount of spiritual life. Hence access to Sacred Scripture ought to be open wide to the Christian faithful.'[5]

**The rediscovery of the place of the Bible in the Church's life, together with the liturgical movement, was one of the great graces God gave the Catholic Church in the twentieth century.** Fr Raymond Brown, the great American Catholic biblical scholar, divided that century into three periods as far as the Church's response to the growth in biblical scholarship was concerned. The first part of the century was marked by a degree of suspicion of scholarship. The second, inaugurated by Pius XII's encyclical *Divino Afflante Spiritu* (1943), encouraged the application of the fruits of that new scholarship to priestly training. The third, beginning with Vatican II, sought to bring the biblical renewal into the bloodstream of the universal Church. While it is a task that remains unfinished, the Bible has once again become a 'book for Catholics'. In the address to the deacons of Rome quoted above, Pope Benedict told them: 'Many of you work in offices, hospitals and schools: in these contexts you are called to be servants of the Truth. By proclaiming the gospel, you will be able to convey the word that can illumine and give meaning to human work, to the suffering of the sick, and you will help the new generations to discover the beauty of the Christian faith. Thus you will be deacons of the liberating Truth, and you will lead the inhabitants of this city to encounter Jesus Christ.'[6]

## The Deacon as a Hearer of the Word

**Fundamental to whatever way he serves the word through his ministry is the deacon's personal engagement with it. 'Believe what you read, teach what you believe, and practice what you teach':** we return again to the bishop's charge to the new deacon, this time noticing how it commits the deacon to building a profoundly personal relationship with the word. A fine collect from the Anglican tradition summarises the centrality of the word in the lives of all believers:

> Blessed Lord, who hast caused all holy Scriptures to be written for our learning; Grant that we may in such wise hear them, read, mark, learn, and inwardly digest them, that by patience, and comfort of thy holy word, we may embrace, and ever hold fast the blessed hope of everlasting life, which thou hast given us in our Saviour Jesus Christ.[7]

Five verbs in this prayer summarise an attitude of receptivity to the word – hear, read, mark, learn, digest. It is a sketch of the attitudes of receptivity that are central to the ancient prayer tradition of *lectio divina*. **Engagement with the daily bread of the** word, especially with the texts that will be proclaimed in the course of the liturgy, should be a central element in the prayer life of the deacon and his family.

Replying to a question posed by a deacon during a general meeting with the clergy of the diocese of Rome, Pope Benedict XVI recounted an anecdote about Pope Paul VI. Paul was deeply moved by the ritual of enthroning the word by the deacon at the beginning of each working day of Vatican II. He asked those responsible for the council's liturgy if perhaps, on some occasion, he might have the privilege of enthroning the Book of the Gospels. No, he was told, he was Pope and this was a deacon's job! He confided his disappointment to his diary, noting, ' ... but I am also a deacon, I continue being a deacon, and I would like to also exercise this ministry of the diaconate placing the Word of God on its throne.' Pope Benedict continues: 'This liturgical enthroning of the Word of God each day during the Council was always for us a gesture of great importance: it told us who was the true Lord of that assembly; it told us that the Word of God was on the throne and that we exercise our ministry to listen and to interpret, to offer to the others this word.'[8] Enthroning the word is the task of deacon, priest and bishop. It is not merely an act of ritual. It is an act of faith in the word's power to transform and to comfort.

NOTES
1  See *General Introduction to Roman Lectionary* (revised edition, 1981), par. 55.
2  Ibid., 60.
3  Pope Benedict XVI, Address to the Deacons of Rome, 16 February 2006.
4  *Catechism of the Catholic Church*, prologue, par 4.
5  Ibid., 131.
6  Benedict XVI, Address to the Permanent Deacons of Rome, 18 February 2006.
7  *Book of Common Prayer*, Collect for Second Sunday of Advent.
8  Benedict XVI, Meeting with the Clergy of Rome, 7 February 2008.

Pádraig J. Corkery

# Christian Discipleship and Catholic Social Doctrine

> This is not a marginal interest or activity, or one that is
> tacked on to the Church's mission, rather it is at the very
> heart of the Church's ministry of service: with her social
> doctrine the Church 'proclaims God and the mystery of
> salvation in Christ to every human being ...' (*Compendium
> of the Social Doctrine of the Church* 67).

Strong words indeed! At the heart of the Christian life is the
invitation to allow the person of Christ and the vision of the gospel
to give direction to our lives. It is a call to allow the gospel to give
shape to our imagination, to our choices and priorities. The life of
Christ recorded in the gospels highlights the importance of values
such as love of neighbour, compassion, forgiveness and justice. We
are left in no doubt that the great commandment 'love of God and
love of neighbour' cannot be watered down or reinterpreted. The
parables of the Good Samaritan and the Prodigal Son, amongst
others, invite and challenge everyone to become a particular kind
of person: compassionate, loving and forgiving. Our response to
the person of Christ and the call of the gospel is to be lived out
in our daily lives. We are called to 'do likewise' and engage with
those who people our lives and especially those who are vulnerable
or on the margins, in ways that are respectful of their dignity, by
being caring and compassionate.

The Christian family is called to make a difference in the
world: to be the 'salt of the earth and the light of the world'.
**We are called to engage with the world we inhabit and to bring the
values and vision of the gospel into our homes and workplaces as
well as into the world of politics, economics and social policy.** This
challenge to transform ourselves and the world by gospel values

is an ongoing and exciting task. It represents a clear rejection of a dualism that would encourage indifference or hostility to our 'neighbour' and the world. For the person of faith 'there cannot be two parallel lives in their existence: on the one hand, the so-called "spiritual life", and on the other, the so-called "secular life", that is life in a family, at work, in social relationships, in the responsibilities of public life and in culture.'[1] Faith and life are meant to be integrated. **This call to be a transforming presence in the world is addressed to all members of the Christian family but has a particular urgency for those called to a ministry of service in the Church such as the diaconate.**

The summons to bring the values of Christ to bear on our world is the source and inspiration for the ongoing development of Catholic social doctrine. The social encyclical *Caritas in Veritate* is the most recent in a line stretching from Pope Leo XIII's *Rerum Novarum*, a tradition that strives to examine and critique the political, social and economic realities of the day from the perspective of the gospel. The Church's social teaching strives to ensure that the communities we inhabit and the economic and social policies we construct are at the service of the human person and are humanised by love and the virtue of solidarity.

The gospel message places the human person at the very centre of its narrative. Commenting on the economic crisis Pope Benedict XVI insists 'that the primary capital to be safeguarded and valued is man, the human person in his or her integrity: "Man is the source, the focus and the aim of all economic and social activity."'[2] The Christian tradition makes bold claims about the person that have important implications for how, at a personal level, we engage with those who people our lives and, at a societal level, how we organise our societies. The Christian claim that all persons are created 'in God's image' is a very profound one that has consequences for how we understand and treat ourselves and others. The first implication of this Christian anthropology is that we each have a dignity that is intrinsic to us. We do not have to earn our dignity nor is it bestowed on us by our family or the state. It is not dependant on our wealth, health or ethnic origin. It is ours because of our nature as sons and daughters of God. Our natural dignity as persons should be affirmed and protected by the state in its duty to the common good of society. A second implication is the recognition of the radical equality of persons. All persons – not just Christians or the virtuous – are created in 'God's image' and possess an inalienable dignity. Finally, Christian anthropology insists that there is more to the human person than the eye can see. Created in the 'image of God' we are more than one-dimensional. There is a transcendent or 'Godly dimension' to every person that needs to be recognised and nurtured. How we understand the human person has important implications for the economic, social and political realms. An inadequate anthropology will lead to decisions and policies that are ultimately to the detriment of the person and community.

The Christian vision of life – how it understands the world – has always included an understanding of human sinfulness and finitude. The biblical account of the Fall provides a realistic understanding of the reality of being human. It is worth noting that the Genesis account records the aftermath of Adam's disobedience in relational terms. The relationships of respect and mutuality between God and humankind, Adam and Eve, and humankind and the created world are ruptured. Discord and shame replace harmony and mutuality. The tradition also recognises that the everyday sins of greed, injustice and indifference can transcend our personal relationships and become enshrined in the very fabric of society. They can become part of the structures, policies and ethos of a particular society. Economic and social policies are human constructs; the result of human choices, values and priorities. As such they can reflect the best of humanity: caring, inclusive and just; or the worst: indifference to the plight of others, self-serving and excluding. The language of 'social sin' or 'structures of sin' is used to describe this latter reality. Though sin is always a personal act, we can talk, in an analogous sense, about systems that are sinful. **What is important to recognise is**

**that unjust systems are maintained by human choices – active support, passive complicity, or indifference.** This was clearly and forcibly brought to the fore by Pope John Paul II:

> – such cases of social sin are the result of the accumulation and concentration of many personal sins. It is the case of the very personal sins of those who cause or support evil or who exploit it; of those who are in a position to avoid, eliminate or at least limit certain social evils but who fail to do so out of laziness, fear or the conspiracy of silence, through secret complicity or indifference; of those who take refuge in the supposed impossibility of changing the world.[3]

In the face of this reality of personal and social sin the tradition has always maintained that change and conversion are possible at both levels. Personal lives and the structures of the world – economic, social and political – can be transformed so that they are more in keeping with the ethos of the gospel. The power of the gospel to change hearts and minds generates a hope and an optimism that is reflected in the dedication of Catholic agencies and individuals as they strive to make our world more attentive to the needs of each *imago Dei*.

Catholic social teaching developed over time as the Church brought the values and insights of the gospel to bear on the economic, social and political spheres. Because we live in a changing world there is a dynamic and unfinished character to the Church's social doctrine. New situations – for example the current economic crisis – bring to light new insights and help clarify or modify older ones. The first social encyclical *Rerum Novarum* (1891) engaged with the plight of workers in the changing landscape of the late nineteenth century. Pope Leo XIII staunchly affirmed and defended the dignity and rights of workers against the prevailing ethos that viewed labour as a commodity to be bought and sold. His defence of the 'just wage', over the 'agreed wage', was confirmed and expanded by later popes. Later encyclicals built on the solid foundation constructed by Leo XIII when they examined the challenges of their times – unemployment, globalisation, development and the ecological crisis – from the perspective of the gospel.

Despite the evolving and dynamic nature of Catholic social doctrine, it is possible to identify central principles that are foundational and unchanging. The *Compendium of the Social Doctrine of the Church* identified the following core principles:

## The common good
**The common good is understood in the Church's social doctrine to be 'the sum total of social conditions which allow people, either as groups or individuals, to reach their fulfilment more fully and more easily'.** It provides the context or environment that enables people to blossom and achieve their potential. This principle provides a robust critique of rugged individualism. It understands the person as a 'person-in-community' and moderates the exercise of individual freedom by appealing to the well-being of others and the community. Everyone in society has a responsibility towards the common good but the political community has a unique and indispensable role. It is important that the content of common good be understood in a wholesome way that includes its transcendent dimension. Christian anthropology, as highlighted earlier, understands the human person as more than one dimensional; God is our origin and destiny and a relationship with God is an essential requirement of the human person. To reduce the common good to socio-economic well-being would not contribute to or enable human flourishing. The human drive to seek religious truth and to live by that truth must be included in any adequate understanding of the common good. Secondly, the common good must be understood in its global dimensions. Individual nations and communities must pursue the common good of the whole human family and not just that of a particular society or people. This perspective – the global common good – provides the ultimate critique of economic and social policies pursued by national and international bodies.

## The universal destination of the world's goods

A fundamental principle of the Christian world-view is that God created the world for everyone. All persons, created in the 'image of God', have been gifted with God's creation. *Gaudium et Spes* states that, 'God destined the earth and all it contains for all of humankind so that all created things would be shared fairly by all under the guidance of justice tempered by charity.'[4]

Over thirty year later, Pope John Paul II in *Centesimus Annus* affirmed this principle:

> God gave the earth to the whole human race for the sustenance of all its members, without excluding or favouring anyone. This is the foundation of the universal destination of the earth's goods.[5]

Because the world was created for the benefit of all, each person has a right to use the goods of the earth. The scope of this right is determined by our needs. Each person 'must have access to the level of well-being necessary for his or her full development'.[6] The right to use the earth's resources is a natural right, inscribed in human nature, and not merely a positive right. It is intrinsic to the human person. It means that all other rights 'including property rights and the right of free trade must be subordinated to this norm [the universal destination of goods]; they must not hinder it, but must rather expedite its application.'[7] The Catholic tradition has 'never recognised the right to private property as absolute and untouchable. On the contrary – the right to private property is subordinated to the right to common use, to the fact that goods are meant for everyone.'[8]

## The principle of subsidiarity

This principle states that the state should not take to itself functions and roles that the individual person and organisations within society can do for themselves. It recognises that families, groups and associations – sports, cultural, political, social – make a necessary and invaluable contribution to the life of society. In this they should be encouraged and supported. The role of the state should be to help (*subsidium*) rather than replace or control these groups and organisations as they contribute to the richness and vibrancy of life in society. The principle was identified in *Quadragesimo Anno* in 1931 as a most 'important principle of social philosophy'. Pope Pius XI was alert to the danger of the individual and social groups being absorbed by the all-powerful state. The content of the principle is that the initiative, freedom and responsibility of the individual and the smaller essential cells in society must not be supplanted. **Underlying the principle is the recognition that 'every person, family and intermediate group has something original to offer to the community'.**[9]

The principle does not, of course, exclude the intervention of the state in the life of society. It provides, rather, a principle of balance that ensures that the individual and groups in society are not denied their rightful freedom, initiative and responsibility while at the same time acknowledging the role of the state in promoting the common good of society. The state must at times take a more proactive and central role in the life of society, for example, by stimulating the economy or creating equality when these projects are unable to be realised by individuals and civil society on their own.

### Participation

Participation in society is seen as a basic right and a duty of all towards the common good of society. It is closely linked to the principle of subsidiarity and could be seen as an inevitable consequence of that principle. It is understood as **'a series of activities by means of which the citizen contributes to the cultural, economic, political and social life of the community to which they belong'.**[10] The Church's social doctrine is critical of totalitarian or dictatorial regimes because 'the fundamental right to participate in public life is denied at its origin, since it is considered a threat to the State itself'.[11] Because participation is a basic right that contributes to the common good of society, there is a duty on all to challenge attitudes and structures that work against participation. Voting is an obvious and essential way for the citizen to participate in the life of society. Through voting in a conscientious way the citizen assumes moral responsibility for the common good of society. In this regard abstaining from voting must be seen as a dereliction of duty.

## Solidarity

In the Church's social doctrine solidarity is understood both as a social principle and a moral virtue that strives to make the oneness of our humanity the foundation for shared action for the betterment of all peoples. It challenges us to engage the structures of sin that perpetuate injustice. These must be transformed into structures of solidarity that facilitate the development of all human beings. This transformation can be achieved by the modification of laws, market regulations and juridical systems so that they enable justice, inclusion and integral human development to be a reality for all. Solidarity is not just a feeling of vague compassion or shallow distress at the misfortunes of so many people. **Rather it involves a firm determination to commit oneself to 'the good of all and of each individual, because we are all really responsible for all.'**[12] Christians in embracing the virtue of solidarity as a response to our shared humanity are further inspired by the example of Christ who calls us to see our neighbour as a 'living image of God' and as Christ in our midst.

## The fundamental values of social life: truth, freedom, justice and love

Catholic social doctrine has identified four pillars on which to build a society that is at the service of the human person and community. The first of these is truth. It is part of the human condition to seek the truth about the reality we call life. There are fundamental questions about life and its meaning that engage people from an early age. This searching is an essential dimension of being human. **Consequently, all persons have the right and duty to search for and live by the truth, and this right must be recognised and facilitated by the state in its service of the human person.** The Christian tradition claims that there are objective truths about reality that can be known and which provide solid foundations for individual and social life. Society should encourage the search for and discussion about these truths.

Despite a sluggish start the Church now recognises freedom as an essential demand of human dignity. It is the highest sign of our creation in the 'divine image'. Through the exercise of our freedom we give shape and direction to our lives. **The *Compendium* gives a list of freedoms that flow from our nature as human beings. These include the right to express our religious, cultural and political ideas, and the right to choose one's state in life.** Freedom, like other rights exercised in society, is not an absolute right and therefore can be restricted. In the first instance we are called to be responsible moral agents and to exercise our freedom with due regard to the rights of others and the moral law. The state, in its service of the community, also has a legitimate role in placing limits on the exercise of freedom – including religious freedom – when such exercise endangers the common good of society.

Justice is the third pillar on which wholesome living – personal and social – is built. **It involves seeing the 'other' as a person with rights and entitlements that require a respectful response from us.** Finally, love is the last element of an adequate foundation for life in society. Love presupposes and transcends justice. Justice must, so to speak, be 'corrected' by that love which, as St Paul proclaims, 'is patient and kind'. It must also possess the characteristics of that merciful love that is at the heart of the gospel. The history of humanity clearly indicates that no legislation, system of rules or negotiation is ever adequate to persuade individuals and nations to live in unity and peace. **Only love can ultimately transform persons, change attitudes and renew societies.**

Despite the vast corpus of social doctrine published by the Church – both universal and local – the reality is that such teaching is unknown by many or often misunderstood. This is acknowledged by the Church itself: 'This doctrinal patrimony is neither taught nor known sufficiently, which is part of the reason for its failure to be suitably reflected in concrete behaviour.'[13] The reasons for this lack of awareness of and appreciation for Catholic social doctrine are complex and beyond the scope of this chapter. Because of this lack in the lives of so many people of faith, **there is an urgent need now to make this rich tradition better known so that it may motivate action for the evangelisation and humanisation of temporal realities. This invitation and challenge is addressed to all believers but is particularly relevant for those called to serve as deacons in the Church.** Deacons can play a prophetic role in both proclaiming and living the truths of Catholic social doctrine in their parishes and communities. In this role they should draw inspiration and courage from the central role given to such doctrine in the Church's self-understanding: '[Social Doctrine] is an essential part of the Christian message, since this doctrine points out the direct consequences of that message in the life of society and situates daily work and struggles for justice in the context of bearing witness to Christ the Saviour.'[14]

NOTES

1 *Compendium of Social Doctrine of the Church* 546.
2 Benedict XVI, *Caritas in Veritate* 25, quoting *Gaudium et Spes* 63.
3 John Paul II, *Reconciliatio et Paenitentia* 16.
4 *GS* 69.
5 John Paul II, *Centesimus Annus* 31.
6 *Compendium of Social Doctrine of the Church* 172.
7 Ibid.
8 Ibid., 177.
9 Ibid., 187.
10 Ibid., 189.
11 Ibid., 191.
12 Ibid., 193.
13 Ibid., 528.
14 Ibid., 67.

Patrick Jones

# Deacon – Minister of the Altar

The deacon is a minister of the Church's liturgy celebrated at the altar. In reflecting on the deacon as minister of the altar, an initial comment might be made so that the importance of the altar is noted. The altar is the essential and permanent focus that attracts our attention when we gather for worship but it also remains outside of that worship. Traditionally we speak of the altar as a sign of Christ himself, often summed up as 'The altar is Christ'. The altar is the place of sacrifice and the table around which the community gathers in worship. The *Rite of the Dedication of an Altar* states that it is both 'a unique altar on which the sacrifice of the cross is perpetuated in mystery throughout the ages until Christ comes' and 'a table at which the Church's children gather to give thanks to God and receive the body and blood of Christ.'[1] The deacon, a minister of the liturgy celebrated at the altar, is, first and foremost, a servant of Christ, through whom, with whom, and in whom, all glory and honour is given to God.

The deacon is a member of that worshipping community gathering around the altar, taking part in the liturgy because it is our common baptismal right and duty.[2] But as a servant of the Church's liturgy he is a minister of that assembly. While all his tasks may be fulfilled by the priest and most of his tasks may be done by a layperson, **the deacon through ordination brings a richer expression to our liturgy.** In the words of Pope Paul VI, who restored the Permanent Diaconate, the diaconate is an expression of the needs and desires of the Christian communities, a driving force for the Church's service or *diakonia* toward the local Christian communities, and a sign or sacrament of the Lord Christ himself, who 'came not to be served but to serve' (Mt 20:28).[3]

The document on the restoration of the Permanent Diaconate outlined succinctly the liturgical ministry of the deacon:

· to assist the bishop and the priest during liturgical actions in all things which the rituals of the different orders assign to him;

· to administer baptism solemnly ...;

· to reserve the Eucharist and to distribute it to himself and to others; to bring the Eucharist as Viaticum to the dying; and to impart to the people benediction with the Blessed Sacrament with the sacred ciborium;

· in the absence of a priest, to assist at and to bless marriages in the name of the Church ...;

· to administer sacramentals and to officiate at funeral and burial services;

· to read the sacred books of Scripture to the faithful and to instruct and exhort the people;

· to preside at the worship and prayers of the people when a priest is not present;

· to direct the Liturgy of the Word, particularly in the absence of a priest.[4]

**The ministry of the altar is about a great variety of liturgies. An understanding of these liturgies and their celebration must be based on a study of the liturgical books.**

## At Mass

The *General Instruction of the Roman Missal* is the principal introductory material placed at the front of the *Roman Missal*. It sums up the role of the deacon at Mass:

> **After the priest, the deacon, in virtue of the sacred Ordination he has received, holds first place among those who minister in the Eucharistic Celebration. For the sacred Order of the diaconate has been held in high honour in the Church even from the time of the Apostles.** At Mass the deacon has his own part in proclaiming the gospel, in preaching God's word from time to time, in announcing the intentions of the Prayer of the Faithful,

in ministering to the priest, in preparing the altar and serving the celebration of the Sacrifice, in distributing the Eucharist to the faithful, especially under the species of wine, and sometimes in giving directions regarding the people's gestures and posture.[5]

The *General Instruction of the Roman Missal* outlines the deacon's ministry at the celebration of the Eucharist.[6] The deacon, wearing the diaconal vestments:[7]

· assists the priest and remains at his side;
· ministers at the altar, with the chalice as well as the book;
· proclaims the gospel and, at the direction of the priest celebrant, may preach the homily occasionally, according to circumstances;[8]
· guides the faithful by appropriate introductions and explanations, and announces the intentions of the Prayer of the Faithful;
· assists the priests in distributing Communion, and purifies, and arranges the sacred vessels;
· as needed, fulfils the duties of other ministers himself if none of them is present.

This ministry is then explained in detail under the heading 'Mass with a Deacon'.[9] A summary shows the fuller expression of the liturgy that we share in through the exercise of the diaconate at Mass.

The deacon may carry the Book of the Gospels in procession at the beginning of Mass. After placing the Book of the Gospels on the altar, together with the priest, he venerates the altar with a kiss. If incense is used, the deacon assists the priest and again the altar is venerated.

Proclaiming the gospel is the high point of the Liturgy of the Word and it is the deacon who is its ordinary reader. In a more solemn form of celebration, the deacon, after receiving a blessing from the priest celebrant, takes the Book of the Gospels and processes to the ambo, accompanied by servers with the thurible and candles. Then, after incensing the Book of the Gospels, he proclaims the reading. The homily is ordinarily given by the priest but on occasion he may entrust it to the deacon.

The Liturgy of the Word concludes with the Prayer of the Faithful. After the introduction by the priest, it is the deacon who normally announces the intentions for which the assembly is invited to pray. If the task of preparing this prayer has been entrusted to the deacon, care should be taken so that the prayer would, as a rule, include 'petitions for the holy Church, for civil authorities, for those weighed down by various needs, for all men and women, and for the salvation of the whole world'.[10]

The deacon prepares the altar assisted by the servers. He assists the priest in receiving the people's gifts of bread and wine and prepares the chalice, adding a little water and presenting it to the priest. If incense is used, the deacon may incense the priest and people. He stands beside the priest at the Eucharistic Prayer and may assist him with the chalice or the Missal. At the doxology at the end of the prayer, he holds the chalice elevated while the priest elevates the paten with the host until the people have responded with the acclamation 'Amen'.

At the prayer and the priest's greeting at the Rite of Peace, the deacon invites all to exchange the sign of peace.

At Communion the deacon receives under both kinds and then assists in distributing Communion to the people. If Communion is given under both kinds, he administers the chalice.

At the Concluding Rites, the deacon invites the people to bow their heads if a Prayer over the People or a solemn formula of blessing is used. After the priest's blessing the deacon dismisses the people with one of the formula of the Missal such as 'Go, in peace, glorifying the Lord by your life'.

Many other liturgies, such as marriage and funerals, include Mass. During the Mass the deacon's role is as above.

## Minister of Holy Communion

Many lay people, as extraordinary ministers of Holy Communion, assist in the distribution of Communion at Mass and also to the sick and house-bound. However, 'it is, first of all, the office of the priest and the deacon to minister Holy Communion to the faithful who ask to receive it'.[11] The deacon is also a minister of Holy Communion brought to the dying as Viaticum.

## Eucharistic Adoration

Again, the priest and deacon are the ordinary ministers for the Exposition of the Blessed Sacrament. As a time of prayer, it directs the attention of the people to the worship of Christ the Lord. 'This liturgy extends the praise and thanksgiving offered to God in the Eucharistic Celebration to the several hours of the day; it directs the prayers of the Church to Christ and through him to the Father in the name of the whole world.'[12] The deacon places the Blessed Sacrament in a monstrance and a period of prayer, song and readings begins. Part of the Liturgy of the Hours may be used. At its conclusion, the deacon takes the monstrance and blesses the people.[13]

## Liturgy of the Hours

At ordination, the deacon is asked: 'Do you resolve to maintain and deepen the spirit of prayer that is proper to your way of life and, in keeping with this spirit and what is required of you, to celebrate faithfully the Liturgy of the Hours with and for the People of God and indeed for the whole world?' In giving an affirmative response to this question **the deacon includes the Liturgy of the Hours as a key element in the spirit of prayer that marks his life and ministry.** There will be many opportunities to celebrate this prayer with others. These occasions may be arranged for special times, for example, during Advent and Lent, but increasingly Morning and Evening Prayer will be seen as the best option on weekdays when the Mass is not celebrated. (Another option is a celebration of the Liturgy of the Word and this is described elsewhere. This option may include the distribution of Holy Communion, when authorised by the bishop.)

## Baptism

Although anyone may baptise in a case of necessity, the ordinary ministers of baptism are bishops, priests, and deacons. The deacon may also have a pastoral and catechetical role in the preparation of the parents and godparents of infants and with adults who are preparing for the Sacraments of Initiation through the Rite of Christian Initiation of Adults.

The Rite of Baptism for Children includes the rites by which a deacon baptises an infant. The deacon may also act as an assistant to a priest who is baptising. This should not be a matter of dividing the rites between them but should respect the role of the deacon as the one who proclaims the gospel, guides the assembly through brief instructions and explanations, and announces the intentions of the intercessions.

## Marriage

Usually it is a priest who assists at weddings but a deacon may be delegated to do so, especially if the celebration of the marriage is outside of Mass or if he is related to the bride or groom.

The deacon must fulfil all requirements regarding delegation as given in canon law as well as the civil requirements regarding the solemniser or officiant.

## Other Sacraments

Deacons do not minister the sacrament of Anointing of the Sick but they are authorised to bring Holy Communion to the Sick and Viaticum to the dying.

In the celebration of Confirmation, the Rite of Reconciliation with several penitents, and the Ordination Rites, the deacon acts as assistant to the bishop or priest since he is not a minister of these sacraments.

## Funeral Rites

In one simple sentence the *Order of Christian Funerals* states the ministry of the deacon at funerals: 'When no priest is available, deacons, as ministers of the word, of the altar, and of charity, preside at funeral rites.'[14] It notes that when a priest or deacon is not available, a layperson can preside at the vigil or wake, and at the rite of committal. **However, as minister of word, altar, and charity, the deacon expresses fully the responsibility of the Christian community to pray for the dead, to offer worship, praise and thanksgiving for the gift of a life now returned to God, and to be part of a ministry of consolation to the bereaved.**

At the funeral Mass, 'the central liturgical celebration of the Christian community for the deceased',[15] the deacon ministers in the usual way.

The Vigil, which might be celebrated in the home of the deceased, in the funeral home, or in the church, takes the form of the Liturgy of the Word. It may also take the form of Morning or Evening Prayer from the Office of the Dead. It is regarded as the principal rite celebrated by the community in the time following the death and before the funeral liturgy. Though not common in this country, it offers the community the opportunity to keep watch with the family in prayer, hearing the Word of God as the source of faith and hope, as light and life in the face of darkness and death and calling on the Father of mercy to receive the deceased into the kingdom of light and peace.

The rite of committal is the conclusion of the funeral rites when the body of the deceased is brought to the cemetery or crematorium. Again it is a moment of separation in the lives of the mourners and the beginning of a new relationship based on prayerful remembrance, gratitude and the hope of resurrection and reunion. The deacon may be the minister of this short but poignant liturgy.

The *Order of Christian Funeral* provides prayer moments for the family, for example, when they gather in prayer after the death. The deacon, underlining his ministry of charity, might lead these prayers.

## Blessings and Popular Devotions

Some blessings are reserved to the ministry of the bishop and priest but many blessings may be assigned to the deacon 'because, as the minister of the altar, of the word, and of charity, the deacon is the assistant of the bishop and the college of presbyters'.[16] If a priest is present it is more fitting that the office of presiding be assigned to him and that the deacon assists.

The deacon may also be the leader of prayers and devotions; for example, the Way of the Cross and, as mentioned above, Exposition of the Blessed Sacrament.

## Conclusion

The assembly gathered around the altar is a powerful and visible sign of the assembly as celebrant of worship. That celebration is given a fuller expression by the variety of ministries and the distribution of duties. The presence of the deacon is one such enrichment.

**In exercising the liturgical ministry of word and sacrament, alongside the ministry of charity, the deacon receives his true identity as a minister of Christ, not simply acting as a substitute or discharging duties that normally are entrusted to others who are not ordained.**

All involved in the training of deacons and associated with their ministry, and the deacon himself, must understand the principles of liturgy and the art of celebrating liturgy well.

NOTES
1 *Rite of the Dedication of an Altar* 4.4.
2 See *Sacrosanctum Concilium* 14.
3 *Ad Pascendum.*
4 *Sacrum Diaconatus Ordinem* 22.
5 *GIRM* 94.
6 Ibid., 171.
7 The vestment proper to the deacon is the dalmatic, worn over the alb and stole. The dalmatic may, however, be omitted out of necessity or on account of a lesser degree of solemnity (*GIRM* 338).
8 See *GIRM* 66.

9  *GIRM* 172-186.
10 Ibid., 69 and 70-71; see also *Sacrosanctum Concilium* 53.
11 *Holy Communion and Worship of the Eucharist outside of Mass* 17.
12 Ibid., 96.
13 In exposing the Blessed Sacrament, the deacon wears an alb (or soutane and surplice) and stole. In giving the blessing, he wears, in addition, a white cope and humeral veil.
14 *Order of Christian Funerals* 14.
15 Ibid., 150.
16 *The Book of Blessings* 18.

William T. Ditewig

# Seeing the Diaconate with New Eyes

## Introduction

Some years ago I wrote a small article entitled 'The Once and Future Diaconate'.[1] It was a review of several pieces of literature which had appeared on the subject of the diaconate renewed following Vatican II. I believe that a title which reflects both the antiquity of the diaconate as well as its untapped potential for service in the contemporary Church is still appropriate here. Many people, when they think of the diaconate at all, recall the many references to the diaconate in the writings of scripture and the patristic era. Still others wonder what relevance such an ancient office might still have for the Church today; in fact, in light of other changes in the Church – such as rapid growth of lay ministry – perhaps the diaconate today is little more than an anachronism.

It is the thesis of this article that **the renewal of the diaconate was proposed by the Council as part of its overall programme of reform and renewal.** The bishops of the Council, through their discussions, debates and documents, continue to challenge us almost five decades later to an ongoing renewal of how we identify who we are as Church, how that Church worships, and what role the Church plays in the world in which we live and work. In short, as both Popes Paul VI and John Paul II reminded us, what is needed in today's Church is a 'new way of thinking' (*novus mentis habitus*).[2]

There is no getting around it: we need this 'new way of thinking' about many things in our Church today, and it is needed urgently. The needs and demands of the Church today have increased in the decades since the Council, with war, hunger, violence, the economy, cultural tensions around the world – all things that the Council hoped to inspire the Church to address – increasing in scope and intensity daily. If such needs are ever to be addressed, the Church must consider what resources she has to offer an effective response to them. Furthermore, it is more than a question of simply identifying resources themselves; rather, it means that we must approach all of these new-old problems with creativity and fresh ideas, using our resources in new ways perhaps unthinkable one hundred years ago. If this is true in general terms, it is particularly true of our understanding of the ways in which we minister to each other and the world around us.

Vatican II encouraged the laity not only to be involved 'in the world', but also to be co-responsible within Church structures as well. The bishops reclaimed their own sacramental identity as successors of the apostles, taught that the *primum officium* of the ordained was within the realm of evangelisation and catechesis, and within this broader framework they ushered a Permanent Diaconate back onto the stage of ecclesial life after an absence of well over a millennium. If the Church was to adopt a new way of thinking about herself and her role in the modern world in general, the renewal of a diaconate exercised as a permanent state of life requires no less. Further, with this permanent form of diaconal ministry absent from the Latin Church for so long, it stands to reason that few people can come to imagine and understand the diaconate without significant reflection. In this article I will offer some theological and pastoral points as background for ongoing discussions on the renewed diaconate.

## Toward a Theology of Diaconate

Nathan Mitchell, in *Mission and Ministry: History and Theology in the Sacrament of Order*,[3] outlines four central issues that have evolved in our theological tradition about orders. I offer these insights on the sacrament of Holy Orders in general as a matrix against which we may discuss the particular situation of the so-called Permanent Diaconate.

1) *Christians have a fundamental 'right' to ministry.* Edward Schillebeeckx speaks of the fundamental 'apostolic right' of

Christian communities 'to a minister or ministers and to the celebration of the eucharist'.[4] This fundamental right is based on two theological principles: a) ministry itself exists to maintain and strengthen the Church's identity as the community of Jesus; and, b) service (*diakonia*) is an essential element in the definition of Church. Richard McBrien notes further that the Church's mission is characterised by three New Testament concepts: *kerygma, koinonia* and *diakonia*. All three of these elements are essential to the nature of the Church.

2) *Ordination is a public process that includes several essential elements*:
   a) participation by the people (choice, election, consent);
   b) fulfilment of canonical conditions (e.g. attachment to specific Church);
   c) ritual action (laying on of hands and prayer);
   d) vocation (God's choice of candidate discerned and expressed through the community's call to ministry).

Mitchell observes, 'No one of these elements, taken in isolation from all the others, is sufficient to constitute what the Roman Catholic tradition has come to understand as "ordination".'[5]

3) '*The sacrament of Order* (sacramentum ordinis) *cannot be reduced, in Roman Catholic tradition, to "priesthood"*. Nor can ministry itself be reduced to "orders". The ordained are one example within the larger context of ministry, while priesthood is one example within the larger category of sacramental order.'[6] Orthodox theologian John D. Zizioulas has observed that the theological significance of the link between the Eucharist and Baptism/ Confirmation lies in the fact that 'it reveals the nature of baptism and confirmation as being essentially an ordination, while it helps us understand better what ordination itself means ... The immediate and inevitable result of baptism and confirmation was that the newly baptised would take his particular "place" in the eucharistic assembly, i.e., that he would become a layman.'[7] In

other words, the new Christian becomes a member of a particular *ordo* in the eucharistic assembly. It is from this *ordo* that certain members are called to become members of other *ordines* in the eucharistic assembly. The theological significance of this fact is crucial. In common parlance, to be a 'layman' implies one who is not an expert in a field. But in theological terms we should keep in mind that the common *ordo* of all the baptised forms the basis for all other *ordines*. Nathan Mitchell writes: 'Understood in this way, baptism is the primary sacrament of ministry in the Church ... Leadership is a baptismal charism, though not all Christians possess it – and it is this charism that the Church seeks in candidates for ordained ministry. The charism of leadership thus serves as a link between the baptismal call to ministry and the vocation to ordained ministry.'[8]

The rediscovery of baptism as the root of all mission and ministry in the Church is complemented by a second rediscovery that, according to Mitchell, has helped clarify the Church's tradition about ministry and ordination: 'Priesthood cannot monopolise the sacrament of Order ... Pope Paul VI's restoration of the diaconate was a recognition, in principle, that ordained leadership in the Church cannot be restricted to celibate priesthood.'[9] The diaconate represents, Mitchell asserts, those New Testament qualities of ministry which Schillebeeckx describes as 'the apostolic building up of the community through preaching, admonition and leadership.'

The restoration of the diaconate is thus important not because it resurrects an ancient order that had all but faded in the West, but because it affirms the principle that *recognition of pastoral leadership is the fundamental basis for calling a Christian to ordained ministry*. Ordained service in the Church begins not with the acquisition of sacramental powers, but with the baptismal charism of leadership, discerned by the community. Even in the case of priesthood, liturgical presidency is derived from pastoral leadership, not vice versa. As David Power has remarked, 'Presidency of community and presidency of the eucharist require the charism of leadership. They fittingly go together, and history suggests that it was one suited to the former who in fact assumed the latter.'[10]

4) Finally, Mitchell addresses the notion of what has been described as the *indelible character of Order*. Mitchell describes the characteristic this way:

> The sacrament of Order establishes a permanent claim on the ordained person ... The permanence of holy orders results not from some sacral power mysteriously imparted to the ordained, but from the nature of Christian baptism, the community's right to ministry, and the uniqueness of Jesus' priesthood. Rooted in a recognised baptismal charism of leadership, the call to ordained ministry is discerned by the community and ritualised through the laying on of hands and prayer. The result is lifelong servantship of Christ and of the Spirit who unites believers to Christ.[11]

## The Diaconate Within the Context of Orders: Leadership in Service

A central theme which emerges from Mitchell's presentation is the notion of Holy Orders as a sharing in the leadership of Christ in the building up of the community. Orders responds to the apostolic right of the community to pastoral leadership, is celebrated in a public manner for the good of the community, is grounded in baptism, and is a lifelong commitment to service. These characteristics apply to all who share in the sacrament of Holy Orders: bishops, presbyters, and deacons.

Focusing our attention on the diaconate, then, we discover several things. For example, all persons who have been ordained deacons remain deacons; there is no such thing, in theological terms, as a *transitional* deacon. A person who is ordained is committed permanently for service in the public good; ordination is not for the good of the individual nor is it a private matter. A deacon subsequently ordained presbyter or bishop remains a deacon, just as a priest who is ordained bishop remains a priest and deacon. **This 'diaconal' aspect of presbyteral service is frequently overlooked in today's Church, but it ought to serve as an important component in the spiritual life of the priest.**

The deacon, according to tradition in the West, is ordained for three interlocking ministries: word, sacrament, and service. It is important to realise that *each* of these three *munera* is a requirement of diaconal ministry. We cannot say, 'the deacon is ordained for service' and ignore word and sacrament. Just as a deacon who neglects the ministries of service and word, and concentrates solely on the liturgy would be justifiably criticised, so too a deacon who neglects liturgy and word and only performs service should be justifiably criticised. It is, after all, a seeking after balance in ministry which applies. It is the same balance we have come to expect from our priests and bishops as well: a 'liturgical' priest who is not involved in other-than-sanctuary ministry would be criticised, as would a man who never sets foot in a sanctuary. In a useful analogy, ordained ministry, regardless of order, is like a three-legged stool: if the legs of word, worship, and service are not kept even, the stool will fall. This principle is just as important to the diaconal order as it is to the presbyteral and episcopal orders.

What happens when this balance is lost in diaconal ministry? If the deacon is only *liturgical*, then he is simply not needed in the life of the Church. The deacon is perceived by bishops, presbyters, and the community as simply a ritualistic addition to the liturgy whose presence is expected only on more solemn occasions (and maybe not even then). Fear of this exclusively liturgical focus (which is of course a fully justified concern) led, however, to the opposite extreme in many places: the liturgical role of the deacon was *undervalued* to the point that deacons were actually taught that it really was not necessary for them to be competent liturgically 'since this isn't a crucial part of the deacon's ministry'. The result has been a vicious cycle. Deacons were not always taught to be competent liturgically, so even pastors who wished to encourage the deacon's liturgical ministry found themselves not doing so because the deacon was unable to function in a competent and effective manner. The deacon, in fact, frequently became just one more thing the presider had to worry about. This led to the conclusion that the deacon simply was not required or desired in the liturgical ministry.

However, the deacon's liturgical role *is* important because he is supposed to bring to that role the framework of service and evangelisation that are involved in his other ministries of word and service. **The deacon is liturgical because he can help witness liturgically (publicly) to the need for evangelisation and pastoral care.** The deacon is supposed to bring to the altar – for the benefit of the entire community – the realities that he has experienced in the streets. Again, balance is the key: the reason the deacon has an *essential* role in the liturgy is because the deacon also has an *essential* role in word and service. The three *munera* are linked and must be in balance.

The deacon's role as a minister of the word carries a similar responsibility. The deacon is not ordained simply to be just another preacher or proclaimer of the gospel at Mass. He is ordained to preach for the very reason that he is supposed to be the official representative of the Church in service to others. A deacon who never preaches or catechises or evangelises has omitted a crucial aspect of the ministry of Christ for which he was ordained. **The deacon should be bringing a complementary perspective on faith, on world, and on Church, which is brought out through his ministries of service and liturgy.** As a servant-leader, he has a responsibility to catechise. Increasingly the theological literature is describing the deacon's unique role as one of evangelisation. Notice, however, what happens if the deacon focuses *only* on preaching and teaching, without the balancing responsibilities of liturgy and service: he winds up being cut off from the very community he is called to serve. The community will perceive him as a teacher, but not necessarily as one who serves as a link between worship, word, and service. It is this linkage which is vital to the life of the community (cf. *Lumen Gentium* 29).

The deacon's role in service is not merely as a doer, but as a leader. The deacon, however, who only does service work, without doing liturgy and word, is simply a social worker and does not require ordination. The Church's understanding is much deeper than that: **the deacon is not ordained to do social work, but to inspire and lead others to join with him in working for the good of the community.**

In sum, it can be said that all of the problems traditionally hypothesised about the diaconate can and will occur when this proper balance between the triple *munera* is not maintained. Any diaconate formation programme which stresses one part of the ministry over another has doomed the diaconate and the deacons it forms to failure. What has emerged over the last forty years of experience of the diaconate and the formation of deacons is this absolutely essential characteristic of balance between the ministries.

Pastorally, this involves more than formation of deacons; it is a catechetical effort involving the whole community, including presbyters. Consider a couple of examples from the liturgy. If a pastor says, 'Well, I want whoever is going to preach to read the gospel', he is missing the point of why the deacon ought to be proclaiming the gospel in the first place. One could also observe that it is at ordination to diaconate, not to presbyterate, that the ordinand is charged with proclaiming the gospel. Why? Because it is the deacon who *should* be the link between word, worship, and service, regardless of who is actually preaching the homily at that liturgy. Furthermore, it is part of the great diversity of ministries which is supposed to take place at the liturgy. In another example, a presider might say, 'I don't need the deacon at the altar; he just gets in the way, and besides, he doesn't add anything essential to the liturgy'. He too is missing some important theological and liturgical points. The deacon has a unique charism to bring to the liturgy, just as lectors and musicians do. It is not that the deacon is there to supplant other ministry; the deacon adds to the tapestry of ministries which should be a part of every liturgy. Would the presider be allowed to say, 'I'm already up here, so I'll just do the readings; we don't need any lectors anymore?' Just as the other liturgical ministries add their own unique gifts to the celebration, so too does the deacon.

**Ordination to diaconate is ordination into the ministry of Christ.** Ordination conveys a sense of leadership in the *communio* of faith. Just as episcopal ordination involves servant-leadership of a particular Church and presbyteral ordination involves leadership in the parish setting, diaconal ordination involves leadership in service. The deacon is not ordained simply to do service, but to lead in service.

Why is all of this important? First, it is important to remember the unity of the sacrament of Holy Orders. The theological principles which undergird the sacrament apply consistently among the three orders. To treat one order in a purely functional way ultimately erodes the meaning of all the orders. We rightly caution against reducing priests to 'sacramental slot machines', recognising that the value of the presbyteral order is not determined by its functions alone; this also applies to the diaconate. If the diaconate is done right, it is no more a purely 'functional' order than is the presbyterate or episcopate. Second, this helps to illustrate the real potential value of the diaconate. If the diaconate is approached properly, the deacon is an evangeliser to service for the life of the Church; that is, after all, what the deacon is supposed to be, not a glorified altar server or a usurper of ministry. The deacon is an enabler of ministry. Most dioceses charge their deacons with the following standard: **if lay ministry is on the increase in your parish, then the ordained team is doing something right;** if lay ministry is declining, the ordained team is doing something wrong.

## Conclusion

The ultimate question we must answer is whether the diaconate is worth it. There have been and continue to be problems related to the implementation of a renewed diaconate. This should not be unexpected, since the Church's experience with a Permanent Diaconate is so recent. These past and current problems need to be addressed, of course. Nonetheless, we are also charged with looking to the future. Specifically, how can the diaconate help us as we move into that future?

A bishop once declared to his staff, 'If we're going to do the diaconate, we're going to do it right or not at all.' How is this to be done? I suggest the following steps as representative. There are probably many more.

**First, we 'do diaconate right' by selecting those candidates who have the gifts and abilities to be leaders across the whole range of diaconal ministry**: word, worship, and service. If the local Church (i.e. the diocese) selects someone just because he is pleasant and popular, or because he is a deeply spiritual man, but one who lacks the ability to share his faith in a public and professional manner, then the local Church and he are doomed to failure.

**Second, the local Church should approach diaconate with the same energy and commitment it does presbyterate**: half-hearted support means half-hearted performance. Get the best possible selection and formation process going. Use consistent standards and stick by them. The diaconate should be just as 'professional' and 'competent' as the presbyterate. If the phrase, 'the professional judgement of the deacon' seems odd to your ears, then the diaconate is not being done correctly.

**Third, all must recognise that the deacon is not a part-time minister.** One of the unique gifts of the diaconate to the life of the Church is that the deacon operates routinely within the marketplace, the home, and the sanctuary. Regardless of where he is, the deacon is minister. To reduce our understanding of the deacon to purely ecclesial functions neuters the diaconate. It is precisely *because* the deacon has to be self-sufficient within the community that he can – in the name of the Church – be a public and permanent sign of Christ the servant.

Fourth, we must recognise and affirm that the deacon is ordained for service to the entire diocese. Procedures that minimise this fact must be avoided at all costs. It is the bishop and the bishop alone who lays hands on the deacon at ordination. **Therefore it is the role of the bishop to assign the deacon to duties that best reflect the deacon's gifts and the community's needs.** In most cases this means that the deacon will be assigned to a parish or parishes, and certainly a ministerial agreement is desirable upon assignment. But the deacon never 'assigns himself' to a ministry, nor does the deacon initiate a change of assignment. Procedures need to be in place that recognise that it is the bishop who makes diaconal assignments and it is the bishop who changes the assignment. In other words, there should be no substantial difference in assignment policy of deacons or priests; in fact, many dioceses with large numbers of deacons have established Deacon Personnel Boards which fulfil the same function as Priest Personnel Boards.

**Fifth, we should provide a solid framework of spiritual formation, academic preparation and ministerial skills development from the moment an applicant enters formation throughout his active ministerial career.** This is another element of professionalism and competence: that we recognise the need for ongoing development in our lives. Those in ministry are in no less need of such development than anyone else.

I hope this article has been helpful in offering some points for reflection. This is a critical time in the life of the restored diaconate around the world. As the nature and meaning of 'ministry' in general continues to evolve, so too does the nature and meaning of ordained ministry. The once-and-future diaconate is right in the middle of this ongoing transformation. Cardinal Suenens of Belgium, during the discussions on the diaconate at Vatican II, remarked that the Church is entitled to all the graces which the Holy Spirit bestows, and he went on to list the diaconate as one of those wondrous graces. May the grace of *diakonia* fill the Church and enflame all disciples with the spirit of service, a love the gives without counting the cost.

NOTES

1 William Ditewig, 'The Once and Future Diaconate: Notes from the Past, Possibilities for the Future', *Church 20* (Summer 2004), pp. 51–54.

2 See, for example, Pope Paul VI's address at the Gregorian University, Rome, 14 December 1974.

3 Nathan Mitchell, *Mission and Ministry: History and Theology of the Sacrament of Order*, Message of the Sacraments, Vol. 6, Collegeville, MN: Liturgical Press, 1982.

4 Edward Schillebeeckx, *Ministry: Leadership in the Community of Jesus Christ*, trans. John Bowden, New York: Crossroad, 1981, p. 37,

5 Mitchell, *Mission and Ministry*, p. 288

6 Ibid.

7 John D. Zizioulas, *Being as Communion: Studies in Personhood and the Church*, St Vladimir's Seminary: New York, 1985, p. 216.

8 Mitchell, *Mission and Ministry*, p. 301.

9 Ibid., p. 303.

10 Ibid., p. 304.

11 Ibid., p. 308.

Tony Schmitz

# Deacons in the Diocese and the Parish

Last November, as I began to ponder what to say on the subject of this chapter, I made a rare visit to London. One reason for my visit was to attend the Catholic Truth Society Lecture 2009, being delivered on this occasion by Deacon Jack Sullivan of the Archdiocese of Boston. When Deacon Jack began to speak about his miraculous cure from a debilitating and agonising spinal condition through the intercession Cardinal John Henry Newman, I was struck by the precision and thrust of his appeal to the great and soon-to-be beatified educator, pastor, and theologian: 'I thought "Why don't I pray to him?" I said, "Please Cardinal Newman, help me to be well so that I can return to classes and be ordained a deacon".'

## Diaconate Formation and Cardinal Newman

Deacon Jack went on to address an audience of over five hundred, speaking plainly but movingly, from the heart and without a note. He described the dreadful condition from which he suffered; he spoke of how he came to know of Cardinal Newman, of his earnest petition to Newman, not explicitly for a cure, but overtly and unequivocally for miraculous help to allow him to complete his studies leading to diaconal ordination, and of how eventually he received a total and medically inexplicable cure. This miracle has since been recognised by the Holy See and allows Newman to be beatified on a yet to be specified date in September 2010, causing Pope Benedict XVI to break his own rule by coming to Britain in order to preside at this most significant beatification, which may lead to Newman's being declared a Doctor of the Church, and which will recall to our attention his outstandingly profound teaching, elegant writing and plain preaching.

Medical doctors had earlier told Jack that he was on the 'brink of complete paralysis' because his lumbar vertebrae were crushing his spinal cord. He was already three years into his diaconal formation course. 'The surgeon said mine was the worst case he'd seen in seventeen years. I was so despondent, because I had worked hard in my diaconate classes, and now it seemed that I would be unable to return to them. At that moment things were very bleak.'

'If it wasn't for Cardinal Newman's intercession when I was experiencing extremely severe spinal problems, it would have been virtually impossible to complete diaconate formation and be ordained for the Archdiocese of Boston. Nor would I have been able to continue in my chosen profession as a magistrate in our court system to support my family.'

The other most signal comment relevant to our subject made by Jack that evening was in response to a question from the audience. Someone asked him something along the lines of: 'After such an astounding miracle, how possibly could you express adequate gratitude?' Jack replied quite simply, 'My fervent desire is to give all that I have both to my parish ministry at St Thecla's Parish in Pembroke, Massachusetts, and to my prison ministry at the House of Correction in Plymouth, Massachusetts. This best expresses the intense appreciation I have for God's gift and for Cardinal Newman who directs my efforts.'

## Jack's Ministry in Prison and Parish

Jack went on to explain how very involved he is in prison ministry due to his affiliation with courts, law enforcement, and his experience with and knowledge of prison facilities:

> Prison ministry came naturally to me. I have come to know what motivates inmates and how they think. While in formation I expressed a desire to engage in prison ministry, but the Archdiocese automatically assigns deacons to parishes so prison work seemed untenable. But, despite

this, I was eventually assigned to work in the prison. I have been appointed to co-ordinate the Catholic Chaplaincy at Plymouth Prison by the Archdiocese of Boston and am assisted by about fifteen Extraordinary Ministers of Holy Communion, another deacon, and four priests.

I also present RCIA [adult catechetical classes] for inmates every Monday evening from September to April, preparing them for the sacraments of Baptism and Confirmation. It is a most worthwhile and rewarding ministry. Despite all the pain and anxiety that I have experienced throughout these eventful years it has been a deeply spiritual and enriching experience. As a result I have tried to develop a greater degree of trust and confidence in God's merciful providence, surrendering myself to his will day by day.[1]

I came away that evening giving thanks for such a powerful and eloquent witness by a man who quite clearly lives his diaconate in an exemplary way. But I also came away with the thought that apart from the role played by the miracle – miracles being by definition out of the ordinary – the rest of what Jack reported about his difficult journey on the way to ordination as a deacon and the way he exercised his ministry upon ordination was not at all atypical.

**First, I do not know of a single deacon who has not had to struggle to complete the demanding formation programme that prepares a man for ordination to the diaconate**, at least since the revised and justifiably more rigorous requirements as set out in the 1998 *Basic Norms for the Formation of Permanent Deacons* issued by the Congregations for Catholic Education and for the Clergy.[2] It was not always so.[3] Although none have had a trial as extreme as Jack's, I am always filled with admiration for the way the candidates for the diaconate here in Scotland have to find an extra fifteen to twenty hours a week to undertake a distance-learning degree course in Applied Theology – designed by Maryvale Institute and validated by the Open University – as the academic component of their formation programme. Like Jack, most are married and working full-time in secular professional employment. As their Director of Studies on behalf of the Bishops of Scotland Diaconate Commission, I receive from time to time candidates' requests for the deferral of submission of essays on account of serious illnesses in the family and other almost insurmountable obstacles to study and yet their determination to stick with the course is a marvel to witness.

## Assignment to Diocese and Parish

Second, upon successful completion of their formation programme and ordination, the newly ordained deacons are assigned their diaconal work in diocese and parish. Many will be designated a diocesan role as well as a parish ministry. Jack was clearly attracted to prison ministry, this being what his professional experience and talents seemed to indicate. **Wise bishops normally take a deacon's qualifications, skills, and life experience into account when designating assignments after consultation with an ordinand and his spouse.** Any assignment cannot however be taken for granted. It is perhaps precisely in this matter of placement that what is distinctive about the extremely flexible nature of diaconal ministry best finds expression. One of the outcomes of the research undertaken by Collins[4] seems to indicate that what is done by a *diakonos* is done as an agent on a mission for another, on behalf of another, in the name of another, or as emissary or envoy of another. Hence we may note the significance of the Promise of Obedience at the ordination of a deacon just before the solemn Litany of the Saints. A deacon does not just express a willingness to serve, anywhere and anyhow, as a lone ranger as it were, but he is 'taken into service', into the very mission of Christ, mediated through the bishop, whose *diakonia* he comes to share in.[5] Accordingly, it would seems to me to be against the spirit of this feature of the diaconal ministry that a deacon, for whatever reason, good or bad, reached a point of 'tendering his resignation'. Rather, he should more properly in such a circumstance request to be relieved of a charge or assignment, after full and serious discussion with his spouse (and children). And, again, a wise bishop will take into account all considerations proffered for a request for a change of assignment.[6] (The very significant role of spouses, incidentally, deserves a chapter on its own and accordingly is not directly addressed in this chapter.)[7]

As I said, in many but not all cases there is a diocesan (or wider) assignment besides a parish assignment. Thus in our own diocese the Chancellor of the diocese is a deacon. A number are, like Jack Sullivan, prison chaplains. One serves as chaplain to seafarers in the Apostleship of the Sea.[8] Others are designated administrative work, often related to agencies devoted to charitable work. One is trained in and specialises in bereavement counselling. In my own case I worked until my sixty-fifth birthday in April 2009 as the director of the Ogilvie Institute, a catechetical and adult formation centre offering, amongst other things, distance learning courses in conjunction with the Maryvale Institute in the Archdiocese of Birmingham in England. Many would see their secular employment as their principal sphere of influence and service, as lecturers or teachers or bus drivers or consultants or nurses or carers or social workers.[9] I even know a deacon in southern Africa who serves as the Minister of Tourism for his government.

## Deacons in Parish Ministry

It remains almost universally true however that every deacon is assigned to a parish. Here he is rooted liturgically and here he will also exercise his threefold *diakonia* in a way that is visible to the parish: the *diakonia* of liturgy, the *diakonia* of the Word of God, and the *diakonia* of charity. And the balance between the three will vary enormously from deacon to deacon and from parish to parish, according to qualifications and circumstances. **It should also be noted that whilst not necessarily visible to his parishioners, the deacon is exercising his threefold *diakonia* no less in his secular employment, or diocesan or extra-diocesan work** or when praying his Liturgy of Hours with or without his spouse at home. A further significant point is that the meaning of *diakonia* extends to the whole of a deacon's service or ministry and not just to the third *diakonia* of *caritas*. Whilst this last is key to, and in some way distinctive of, diaconal ministry, it is not the whole of his ministry.[10] There are many who argue, and rightly, that deacons should be more involved in a high or low profile way in working for justice and initiating or animating more projects working for justice or attending to those most in need. It is certainly the mind of the Church that deacons should have specialist knowledge of the social doctrine of the Church. They are also called to 'transform the world according to the Christian order'.[11]

## A Threefold Ministry

There is no need whatsoever to erect false oppositions between the three *munera*. At ordination, 'From [Christ] ... deacons receive the strength to serve the people of God in the *diaconia* of liturgy, word and charity, in communion with the bishop and his presbyterate. The ministry in which Christ's emissaries do and give by God's grace what they cannot do and give by their own powers, is called a "sacrament" by the Church's Tradition. Indeed, the ministry of the Church is conferred by a special sacrament.'[12] There will always be a need to recall the third *diaconia* to the attention of bishops, priests, deacons, and layfolk – and even particularly to deacons – but it should never be at the expense of the other two. One sometimes comes across a disparagement of the deacon's liturgical role and tasks. If he is not rooted in the liturgy, and particularly in the Eucharist, he is not a deacon. When I join the team of those who feed the homeless on a Wednesday evening, am I being less or more diaconal than when presenting at the RCIA session which our parish hosts and the deacon leads every Monday of the year? Or is my offering bioethical counsel – assuming I am competent to do so – to a nurse working in reproductive medicine on the boundaries of material and formal cooperation any more or less the work of a deacon than preparing for and celebrating a baptism or presiding at a funeral liturgy and burial? If, with my wife, I run an eleven-week training course for readers or do a refresher course for extraordinary ministers of Holy Communion, is that being less of a deacon than when promoting the Scottish International Aid Fund or Aid to the Church in Need?

## The Spirituality of the Deacon

Everything comes together in the proper understanding of the spiritual life of a deacon. As I was writing these words, news came through of a new Motu Proprio issued by Pope Benedict XVI, *Omnium in mentem*.[13] But whatever the other implications of the slight change of the wording in the Code of Canon Law, the insertion of the new clause in Canon 1009, § 3 is to be welcomed:

> *Qui constituti sunt in ordine episcopatus aut presbyteratus missionem et facultatem agendi in persona Christi Capitis accipiunt, diaconi vero vim populo Dei serviendi in diaconia liturgiae, verbi et caritatis.*

> The minister constituted into the Order of the episcopate or the priesthood receives the mission and power to act in the person of Christ the Head, while deacons receive the faculty to serve the People of God in the diaconates of the liturgy, of the word, and of charity.[14]

I say it is to be welcomed because it emphasises once again what the translation calls the 'diaconate of the liturgy, the diaconate of the word, and the diaconate of charity'. This takes us away from restricting the meaning of *diakonia* to the ministry of charity, an orientation that is German protestant and nineteenth century in origin, as ably demonstrated by Collins.

For these are not three distinct jobs for deacons, each worthy of approximately a third of the deacon's time and energy. 'They are three sides of a triangle, without any one of which there is no triangle; **genuine *diakonia* is always ministry in *all three*** *senses.* **When deacons serve the poor they are preaching and they are practicing what they preach; they are also worshipping by extending the Sacred Liturgy beyond the confines of the Church and the Mass.'** [15] If they assist marginalised people in some charitable way, they may well end up evangelising, catechising, baptising, marrying, or burying them; likewise, if they assist them sacramentally, they will inevitably end up teaching the faith and offering other kinds of pastoral assistance. All three sides of the diaconal triangle are visible and active at once. Diaconal *caritas* is concurrent with diaconal word and worship. Word and worship should propel us to communion not just with the like-minded or those present and happy with the Church, but send us out to those still far from the Church or suffering in any way.

Deacons often debate amongst themselves questions of 'who' and 'where' the poor are today and how we might reach and serve them. Clearly there are still financially or materially poor people (the numbers of genuinely homeless men on the streets of Aberdeen this winter, for example, is disgracefully greater than ever), but there are also other kinds of poverty that cry out for assistance: psychological, emotional, social, educational, cultural, moral and spiritual. As Pope John Paul II observed:

> Certainly *today's world* is not lacking in opportunities for ... the simplest acts of charity or the most heroic witness to the radical demands of the gospel. All around us many of our brothers and sisters live in either *spiritual or material poverty* or both. So many of the world's people are *oppressed by injustice* and the denial of their fundamental human rights. Still others are troubled or suffer from a loss of faith in God, or are tempted to give up hope ... [Deacons] are [properly] involved in *direct service to the needy*: to the ill, the abused and battered, the young and old, the dying and bereaved, the deaf, blind and disabled, those who have known suffering in their marriages, the homeless, victims of substance abuse, prisoners, refugees, street people, the

rural poor, the victims of racial and ethnic discrimination, and many others. As Christ tells us, 'as often as you did it for one of my least brothers, you did it for me' (Mt 25:40).[16]

The fields or arenas of operation for the deacon's threefold ministry in parish and diocese, in the name of bishop and Church, today would include:

· promoting and sustaining the works of SCIAF, CAFOD, Caritas and the Society of St Vincent de Paul, and their equivalents;
· chaplaincy to hospitals and nursing homes, visiting the sick, ministry to the elderly, ministry to the disabled;
· chaplaincy to prisons and prison-visiting and post-release aftercare;
· bereavement counselling (if trained and qualified);
· chaplaincy to the armed services, police, rescue services, maritime services;
· chaplaincy to immigrants;
· school chaplaincy and youth ministry;
· marriage, family and life ministry, including marriage preparation;
· work in (if qualified in canon law), or as auditors for, marriage tribunals;
· coordinating pastoral care at parish, deanery or diocesan or wider level;
· participation in parish, deanery, or diocesan pastoral councils;
· promoting awareness of Catholic social teaching and action for justice, development and peace and the protection of creation/ environment;
· being spiritual advisers to conferences of SVdP, the Legion of Mary or other groups;
· promoting and sustaining the governing activities of the bishop, e.g. by working, if qualified, as chancellors, in tribunals or the bishop's office;
· promoting adult formation in the faith and leading RCIA teams;
· facilitating the development of the full range of lay ministries;
· missionary activity in remote Christian communities.

In fact of course, the list is endless. And it is circumstance, giftedness, and the diocesan bishop, that determine and specify particularities of ministry.

Pope Benedict XVI recently said that **'one characteristic of the diaconal ministry is precisely the multiplicity of its applications ... there is no single profile. What must be done varies according to a person's formation and situation ... [but] charity will continue in every age and every diocese to be key ...'[17]**

## At the Direction of Another

All I do in the parish is at the direction of my young and energetic parish priest who has two parishes to pastor. Recently, after a most successful *Peregrinatio pro Christo* led by a group of fine young and not so young members of the Legion of Mary from Ireland, my parish priest asked me to become spiritual director to the new *praesidium* which has just started up in the parish and which meets for a couple of hours every Thursday of the year, besides doing sterling direct evangelising work going from door to door. He asked me to lead a healing service in his other parish once a month. Now that I am in part-time employment, I assist at every Mass in the parish, Sundays and weekdays, which are preceded by an hour's Adoration and Morning Prayer. The deal is also that he and I take it in turns to preach at Mass, on Sundays and weekdays, alternating each week. Now the flexibility of my working hours makes this possible. This may often not be true of deacons in secular employment. And I know of many deacons, able preachers, whose parish priest jealously guards his right to preach and who rarely gives the deacon an opportunity. It is then that we need to recall Bishop Anthony Fisher's quip in the same address in August last year: 'Table waiters without the tips, that's what you are. Doesn't sound very exalted, I know, unless you've heard Jesus' teaching about authority and service (Mt 20:20-28 and parallels) or the story of him waiting upon his apostles at the Last Supper (Jn 13). His mandate on that last night, to go and do likewise, is the inspiration of the diaconate, both as a sacred order within the Church and as a sacred service in which all the baptised share.'

What the deacon does is always at the direction of Another. He works as the agent on a mission for Another, on behalf of Another, in the name of Another, or as emissary or envoy of Another. And his agency is always mediated, whether explicitly or implicitly, through bishop or pastor. As Saint Benedict wrote in his Rule: 'Put aside your own will so as to go to war under Christ the Lord, the real King, assuming the keen and glittering weapons of obedience.' It is an ecclesial ministry into which the deacon is ordained. As the bishop says when placing the Book of the Gospels in the hands of the newly ordained deacon:

Receive the Gospel of Christ,
whose herald you now are.
Believe what you read.
Teach what you believe,
And practice what you teach.

NOTES

1 Peter Jennings, *Cardinal Newman: The Story of a Miracle*, London: Catholic Truth Society, 2009, p. 50.

2 Congregation for Catholic Education & Congregation for the Clergy, *Basic Norms for the Formation of Permanent Deacons & Directory for the Ministry and Life of Permanent Deacons*, 1998. These are further specified by national norms; for Scotland for example, by *Norms for the Formation of Permanent Deacons in Scotland, Commission for the Permanent Diaconate*, 2007. The Irish Bishops issued *The Permanent Diaconate: National Directory and Norms for Ireland* in 2006.

3 For a brief history of the restoration of the diaconal ministry in its permanency in Scotland and the early days of formation, see the articles by Bishop John Jukes and Deacon John Futers in *A Garland of Silver: A Jubilee Anthology in honour of Archbishop Mario Conti*, Tony Schmitz (ed.), Aberdeen: Ogilvie Press, 2002, pp. 217-235.

4 John N. Collins, 'A German Catholic View of the Diaconate and Diaconia', *New Diaconal Review* 2 (May 2009), pp. 41-46. His original research was first published in *Diakonia: Re-interpreting the Ancient Sources*, Oxford: Oxford University, 1990.

5 See Tony Schmitz, 'The Diaconate: Perspectives on its Development, The International Theological Commission', *New Diaconal Review* 1 (November 2008), pp. 56-57.

6 A *Diocesan Decree of Appointment* is a most useful document to be agreed between bishop, deacon and spouse, and parish priest if it lists broadly the duties and responsibilities and time commitments of the deacon particularly in his parish ministry, so that false expectations may be avoided by all parties, particularly if a deacon remains in secular employment and still has a young family.

7 See Nelleke Wijngaards Serrarens, *Partners in Solidarity: Wives of Deacons*, Arnhem, 2006.

8 See Richard Withers, 'Chaplaincy among Seafarers', *New Diaconal Review* 2 (May 2009), 21-29. See also 'Diakone auf See und in Hafen', *Diaconia* 44 (2009), 12-69.

9 Pope Benedict XVI at a meeting with the Clergy of the Diocese of Rome on 7 February 2008 said he is an enthusiast for the Permanent Diaconate '... because it seems to me that it enhances the riches of the Church's sacramental ministry. At the same time, it can also serve as a link between the secular world, the professional world and the world of the priestly ministry, since many deacons continue to carry out their professions and keep their posts – both important and also simple positions – while on Saturdays and Sundays they work in church. Thus, they witness in the contemporary world as well as in the world of work to the presence of the faith, the sacramental ministry and the diaconal dimension of the sacrament of Order.'

10 On charity as a responsibility of the whole Church and bishops in particular, see Pope Benedict's first encyclical *Deus Caritas est* 21: 'A decisive step in the difficult search for ways of putting this fundamental ecclesial principle into practice is illustrated in the choice of the seven, which marked the origin of the diaconal office (cf. Acts 6:5-6). In the early Church, in fact, with regard to the daily distribution to widows, a disparity had arisen between Hebrew speakers and Greek speakers. The Apostles, who had been entrusted primarily with "prayer" (the Eucharist and the liturgy) and the "ministry of the word", felt over-burdened by "serving tables", so they decided to reserve to themselves the principal duty and to designate for the other task, also necessary in the Church, a group of seven persons. Nor was this group to carry out a purely mechanical work of distribution: they were to be men "full of the Spirit and of wisdom" (cf. Acts 6:1-6). In other words, the social service which they were meant to provide was absolutely concrete, yet at the same time it was also a spiritual service; theirs was a truly spiritual office which carried out an essential responsibility of the Church, namely a well-ordered love of neighbour. With the formation of this group of seven, *"diaconia"*– the ministry of charity exercised in a communitarian, orderly way — became part of the fundamental structure of the Church.' And on applied *caritas*, see his second encyclical wherein the Church's preferential love of the needy is articulated for our times, *Caritas in Veritate*, a document still to be absorbed by deacons and others.

11 See Ashley Beck, 'Encyclical Letter *Caritas in Veritate*', *New Diaconal Review* 3, (November 2009), 56-61, 56: 'To be honest, this is often not the case: in the early days of the Permanent Diaconate, formation programmes did not even

include social teaching.' Many deacons knew as little about social teaching as priests and layfolk.

12 *Catechism of the Catholic Church* 875.

13 For a discussion anticipating the need to change canon 1008 to bring it into harmony with the change in the second (1997, Latin) edition of the *Catechism of the Catholic Church*, which altered the wording of para. 1581 of the first (1992, French) edition of the *Catechism*, see Alphonse Borras, 'Where are we?' *New Diaconal Review* 3, (November 2009), 23–26. See also Didier Gonneaud, 'The Sacramentality of the Diaconate' *New Diaconal Review* 1 (November 2008), 4–17.

14 For the text of the Motu Proprio see http://www.vatican.va/holy_father/ benedict_xvi/apost_letters/documents/hf_ben-xvi_apl_20091026_codex-iuris-canonici_lt.html (accessed 21 December 2009).

15 Bishop Anthony Fisher, unpublished address to the National Conference of Deacons in Penant Hills, Australia, 8 August 2009.

16 John Paul II, Address to Permanent Deacons, Detroit, 19 September 1987, 4 (italics in original). Likewise Benedict XVI, Address to the Permanent Deacons of Rome, 18 February 2006: 'In these years new forms of poverty have emerged. Indeed, many people have lost the meaning of life and do not possess a truth upon which to build their existence; a great many young people ask to meet men and women who can listen to and advise them in life's difficulties. Beside material poverty, we also find spiritual and cultural poverty.'

17 Ibid.

# Bibliography

As well as items mentioned in the notes of the individual chapters, the following is offered as a select bibliography on the Permanent Diaconate.

Barnett, James M., *The Diaconate: A Full and Equal Order*, Minneapolis, MN: Seabury Press, 1987.

Collins, John N., *Diakonia: Re-interpreting the Ancient Sources*, New York: Oxford University Press, 1990.

Cummings, Owen F., *Deacons and the Church*, Mahwah, NJ: Paulist Press, 2004.

Ditewig, William T., *The Emerging Diaconate: Servant Leaders in a Servant Church*, Mahwah, NJ: Paulist Press, 2007.

_____ *101 Questions and Answers on Deacons*, Mahwah, NJ: Paulist Press, 2004.

Echlin, Edward P., *The Deacon in the Church: Past and Present*, Staten Island, NY: Alba House, 1971.

Keating, James (ed.), *The Deacon Reader*, Mahwah, NJ: Paulist Press, 2006.

Osborne, Kenan B., *The Permanent Diaconate: Its History and Place in the Sacrament of Orders*, Mahwah, NJ: Paulist Press, 2007.

*New Diaconal Review* 1 (November 2008). This is a journal dedicated to the Permanent Diaconate published twice a year by the International Diaconate Centre – North European Circle.